LARRY HATTEBERG'S
KANSAS PEOPLE

Dedication

For all your patience
With all my love –
Larry Hatteberg
Wichita, Kansas 1991

Judy Hatteberg and daughters, Sherry, left, and Susan, right.

A portion of the proceeds from the sale of each book goes to
Big Brothers and Sisters organizations throughout Kansas.

LARRY HATTEBERG'S
KANSAS PEOPLE

Editor
Howard Inglish

Photographer
Vada Snider

Jular Publishing
Wichita, Kansas

A Collection of Colorful Personalities from the Sunflower State

Acknowledgments

Associate Editor: Cindy Mines
Writers: Dorothy Belden, Roberta Birk, Howard Inglish and Cindy Mines
Proofing: Les Anderson, Tami Bradley, Larry and Judy Hatteberg, Vada Snider
Typesetting and Page Composition: KPN Typographics, Inc. –
    Randy Powell and Pam Headley
Halftones: KPN Typographics Inc. and Edwards Typographic Service
Printer: Multi Business Press, Hillsboro – Joel Klaassen and Stan Thiessen
Administration: Judy Lonneke and Portia Smith

The advice and assistance of many helped bring this book through 10 months of development to the product you have in your hands.

Jim Hellman, a Wichita State University graphic arts professor, helped refine the design for the book's profile pages and the cover.

Cindy Mines also assisted in this process. In fact, Cindy, associate editor for the book, was involved early on in editing, layout and writing, and played a key role in producing *Larry Hatteberg's KANSAS PEOPLE.*

Randy Powell, president of KPN Typographics, Inc., gave important advice and devoted much energy and countless hours to see the book to its completion. Randy also helped me in the design of the cover, which was done at KPN.

Another person I would like to thank for the patience and expertise she brought to the project is Pam Headley at KPN. Also, thanks to Peggy Schreck, Judy Reimer and the other support people at KPN.

Cindy Saxon, owner of Wordworx Secretarial Service, provided important assistance in the project's early stages.

Portia Smith and Judy Lonneke handled the execution of many of the administrative details, and played a key role in doing so.

Andy West and Carol Duerksen helped in the final phases of production.

Others who provided assistance include: Rex Abrahams, Jan and Larry Cowick, Rhonda Evans of Dillons, Jan McDaniel of KAKE-TV, Nick Mork of Big Brothers & Sisters, Barney Murray and Bill Pfaff of MS News, Sherry McKennee, Betty Jo Peters, Carol Stuck and Susan Wesselowski.

Also for their special advice and encouragement, I would like to thank Deloris Boothe, Randy Brown, Victoria Mork, Mary Wessel and my parents, Charles and Ruth Inglish.

And most of all, I would like to thank Larry and Judy Hatteberg for believing in me.

Howard Inglish, Editor and Project Coordinator

First Edition
Copyright © 1991 by Jular Publishing

Library of Congress Catalog Number: 91-77064
ISBN: 0-9631186-0-9

Editor Howard Inglish

Howard Inglish was born on Sept. 11, 1946, in Okmulgee, Okla. In 1949, his family moved to Del City, where his father took the position of principal of Del City Elementary. Howard graduated from Del City High School in 1964 and attended the University of Oklahoma, majoring in sociology and political science. He began working in college for the *Oklahoma Journal* as a campus correspondent, and later as a general assignment reporter.

In 1969, he moved to Wichita to work for the *Wichita Eagle.* Howard has covered city and state government, business, and local and federal courts for several newspapers,

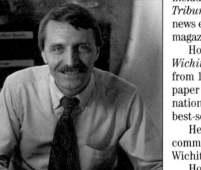

including the *Eagle,* the *Journal,* the *Tulsa Tribune* and the *Wichita Sun,* where he was news editor. He was publisher of the *Wichitan* magazine from 1977 to 1982.

Howard was on the original staff of the *Wichita Business Journal,* and served as editor from 1986 to 1990. During his editorship, the paper won a number of awards at the state and national level. In 1990, he was the editor of the best-selling Kansas book, *Year of the Storms.*

He has served on the boards of several community organizations, including the Wichita Jaycees and Shakespeare in the Park.

Howard's parents, Charles and Ruth Inglish, still live in Del City. Years in Kansas: 16.

Photographer Vada Snider

Vada Snider was born July 24,1958, in Edmonton, Alberta, Canada. She moved to Kansas with her family when her father joined the faculty of Bethel College in 1966. Vada graduated from Hesston High School, and received a degree in English and music at Bethel College in North Newton where she lives today. She also holds a master's degree in communications from Wichita State University. Vada spends winters freelancing in Kansas and summers interviewing music celebrities for *The Chautauquan Daily* in New York.

Vada's photographs for the *Ark Valley News* and the *Wichita Business Journal* have won numerous state, regional and national awards, and her work has appeared in a broad range of publications, including national corporate magazines. Along with her photography career, Vada is a professional flutist, and tours the state through the Kansas Arts Commission Touring Program. Years in Kansas: 25.

How We Did What We Did in This Book

Howard Inglish of Wichita on editing 4,000 years of Kansas living history

Almost exactly one year and more than 700 hamburgers ago, I approached Larry Hatteberg about publishing a book based on his "Hatteberg's People" series on KAKE-TV.

"You want to do a book based on 'Hatteberg's People'?" he said, with a note of questioning and intrigue in his voice. Larry continued, after I explained my vision of how the concept would work, by saying he liked the idea, was pleased I had brought it to him, and that I should get back with him in a month.

We talked briefly again before Christmas – this was during the time I was traveling all over the state to promote the book, *Year of the Storms* – and agreed we would spend some time discussing the idea in late January.

We talked every few weeks, and I knew Larry was getting into the book when he started saying things like, "Well, how would we do this?" and "How are we going to do that?"

I noted that he was using the word "we" and apparently I was providing the right answers. In February, Larry said to go ahead and prepare a budget and book outline. In March, we agreed to give a tentative go for the project. In April, we were finalizing the budget, and we had an important meeting with Bob Wall, president of First National Bank of Conway Springs, and his board of directors.

Once we had their OK, Larry and I intensified the pace of going through the hundreds of "Hatteberg's People" profiles that had aired on KAKE-TV and other stations across the state – including some that had been broadcast nationally. We narrowed the list down to about 120.

By this time, in May, I was well into my 150th hamburger ingested during the project. I also had held meetings with our printer, Multi Business Press of Hillsboro, and began receiving my weekly dose of encouragement and advice from Joel Klaassen, marketing director for Multi Business Press.

I had initial discussions with Vada Snider, one of the state's most recognized print photojournalists, on the concept. Vada had worked for me when I was editor of the *Wichita Business Journal,* and I had a feeling she would like a book based on people, especially Kansas people.

It was, by the way, simply in conversations with Larry and Judy Hatteberg, Vada Snider and Cindy Mines, the book's associate editor, that the name *Kansas People* stuck. It was clear, simple, direct, and those we talked to liked the title.

Vada, like Larry, was especially intrigued with the challenge of turning into print a book based on television profiles.

By mid-May, we had refined our mission statement into a measure we could use to narrow down the list of those who would be in the book. We needed a collection of colorful personalities who reflected the unique character of Kansas. That's where the subtitle came from and also the phrase on the back cover:

"They may be called characters by some, but more importantly, they are Kansans of character."

Once we had 30 of the profiles pinned down, we gave initial assignments to Vada in late May, and she began her travels across the state — travels that were to add 6,000 miles to her odometer.

It was also about this time we began contacting the Big Brothers & Sisters organizations around the state. Larry and I wanted a book about people to benefit a people-oriented community organization — one that had a role in shaping people's character. That is why we chose Big Brothers & Sisters to receive a portion of the proceeds from the sale of each book.

"You want to do a book based on 'Hatteberg's People'?" he said, with a note of questioning and intrigue in his voice.

Larry and I were also seeking diversity in age and in geography. That is why the Kansas People in this book range in age from 13 (Erin Caffrey of Mount Hope) to 97 (Rose Nix Leo of Howard), and live literally from border to border, as evidenced in the profiles on Ed and Cindy Harold of Weskan and on Wolf River Bob Breeze of White Cloud.

Most have lived in Kansas the great portion of their lives, and the average number of years in Kansas is more than 47: the 85 people profiled in the 75 articles represent nearly 4,000 years of Kansas living.

The selection process continued through the summer, Cindy and I began interviews, and writers Dorothy Belden of Wichita and Roberta Birk of Emporia were brought on.

We developed a sample format, and were enthused that the first photographs Vada brought us captured the spirit, character and personality of those profiled.

As the days of summer begin to shorten, my days grew longer. The summer ended with the count at more than 400 hamburgers, and I got a car phone so Larry and I could have phone meetings as we hustled around town. In addition, I adapted the AT&T slogan and learned the art of staying in touch with friends by talking to their answering machines.

Some of the profiles Larry did during the summer were added, and then we were able to complete arrangements to interview Olive Ann Beech of Wichita, a profile we felt brought an added dimension to the book.

Another plus was the interest of the good folks at Dillons Stores Inc. and their agreement to participate in the Big Brothers & Sisters donation.

Now, many who have seen advance publicity on the book have asked me what approach we used to translate the Hatteberg videos into print, and how we did it.

Well, there were many long nights, but how we did the writing is:

The scripts from Larry's interviews served as a model for the profiles. In most cases, a number of the original quotes are included in the profile. The writers updated what has happened to our subjects since the television piece aired. Then, because we wanted to take advantage of what print can offer that television doesn't, I suggested the idea of the "Snapshot Biography," which is attached to each profile. This gives our readers a fuller and richer sense of these Kansas people.

Vada shot all the photographs — except those in the film strips — and our plan from the beginning was to emphasize a portrait photograph on the right-hand page.

To create the photos in the filmstrips, Larry spent countless hours with a camera in front of his VCR, perfecting the technique of shooting still photos off the video. Then Randy Powell of KPN Typographics, Inc. perfected the technique on the scanner of sharpening the film strip photos.

Well, there you have it. It's been an exciting, bumpy and educational ride. I know now all too well the nuances of taste that occur in the hamburgers produced at many of the take-out restaurants in Wichita.

And I've learned a lot, about book publishing and about Kansas People. It has been a lot of fun to have met or talked with many of them, and it has been an honor.

Finally, I would like to thank Larry and Judy Hatteberg for the patience they showed with me and the confidence they expressed in my work.

Larry and I are often asked if we will do another book. Maybe. But Larry, let's wait a couple of years before we do, or at least until I've had a few steaks under my belt.

Howard Inglish / Editor and Project Coordinator
November 1991

Table of Contents
75 Profiles on 85 Kansans of Character

FOREWORD

Small-town streets–where the cottonwoods, birch and maple trees defined the boundaries of my hometown.

It was peaceful there. It was home.

Winfield, Kan., is nestled in the Walnut Valley of Cowley County. Time has always moved slower for me there, as if it were a gift that I should linger over, like a fine wine.

It is the people in this town who first touched me with their lives. Growing up with parents who loved me and with people who gave to the community from their hearts–I heard their stories.

I met Shorty, Rattlesnake Pete and Herk. There was Homer, Bill, Gus and Hoppy. They were all part of my growing-up years. I can still see their faces today–frozen in time and ageless.

My parents, Merle and Mary Hatteberg, gave me a great gift. They showed, through example, that my relationships with people were the only things in life that were truly important.

My father was a baker. Many times I watched as people would go through our trash cans looking for bread that had been tossed aside. When my father saw that, he would give them a fresh loaf right off the shelf.

When they were hungry, my father fed them. Questions were never asked.

My mother was a nurse. Her years of caring for the sick gave me understanding and patience. When people talk about her, they say she was the best nurse they ever had.

That's because she cared. She talked to them. She listened to their problems. She shared her life with them. They weren't numbers in a computer. They were real people with real feelings.

So as I grew older, there was the inevitable process of defining my own life, taking the ingredients taught by my parents and mixing them with life's other spices. It's an experience that we all go through with the help of others.

In 1974, "Hatteberg's People" was born. I had been working for KAKE for 11 years and had received positive feedback from many of my feature stories. A friend in management at KAKE, Ron Loewen, suggested we franchise the segment, give it a name and run the series at a set time in the newscast. He dubbed it "Hatteberg's People" and the name stuck. Since 1974, hundreds of people have been subjects for the series.

"My father was a baker. Many times I watched as people would go through our trash cans looking for bread that had been tossed aside. When my father saw that, he would give them a fresh loaf right off the shelf."

My philosophy is to let the people tell their own stories. Everyone has something to say–but we have to stop and listen. I've found that I do a lot of listening. It's as important for me to learn something from the folks I do stories on as it is for the viewer. If I'm learning, then it's an accurate assumption the viewer is too.

Television is a window to the soul. The personal nature of the television image, coupled with the experiences of real people talking directly to the camera, is a powerful way to communicate thoughts and ideas. But most of all, it gives us first-person experiences. The best television transmits that "experience" to the viewer.

I've maintained over the years that reporters aren't very important people. That has met with some criticism from my colleagues. But I view the "Hatteberg's People" segment as a voice of the people. My task, as a reporter, is simply to organize the thoughts of those interviewed into a cohesive story. It is the telling of that story, coupled with powerful creative pictures and sound, that gives the story its power.

A friend of mine, Fred Shook, professor and author at Colorado State University in Ft. Collins, described it this way:

"So often real people speak more eloquently than reporters. They have lived the story after all, and thought about its meaning at personal levels almost inaccessible to the average writer and reporter. Their writing is conversational, perceptive and authoritative."

For the first 10 years, I photographed, edited and wrote all the stories. In the business, I was called a "one-man band." But in 1986 I moved into management at KAKE-TV. The stories continued—I still wrote them, but I let other photographers do the actual shooting.

During the first 10 years, my voice, along with the subject's, was heard on the tapes. Then for a period of nearly two years we experimented with only using the subject's voice, in effect, telling his or her own story. In some cases it worked well and still does. But we found that sometimes it still needed additional writing to explain what the subject didn't or couldn't say. So the format changed back to the original structure.

We still try to use the approach of letting the subject tell his or her own story. I simply fill in lines of copy as needed to amplify or clarify points.

As I think of my parents, I can't help but know their influence is guiding the structure of my stories. Their ever-present sensitivity toward people rubbed off on me in subtle ways. I'm finding that in every story is a piece of my own life.

While many fine photojournalists have contributed to the "Hatteberg's People" segment over the years, I'd like to particularly acknowledge the work of two of those creative people. At KAKE-TV, chief photojournalist Dennis Decker and photojournalist Doug Raines have photographed the bulk of the television stories during the last few years. It is their creative eye that contributes to the power of the images as they flow across the television screen. Without the insight and sensitivity of those individuals, these stories would not be possible.

In this book, the still photographs taken by photojournalist Vada Snider capture the warm feeling and unique qualities of these people that mirror the original television stories. Photojournalism that captures the inner spirit of the subject is an art form only a few understand — and fewer ever master. Vada's sensitivity gives this book its power through images that warm the heart and touch the soul. I am indebted to Vada for her wonderful photography that "freezes" many of the magic moments I've enjoyed with all these people.

This book is the inspiration of a good friend–Howard Inglish. The book was born through his eyes. It was at his suggestion that it is a reality. It was his superior attention to detail, his writing skills and his view that Kansas and its people should be showcased, that brought the book to completion. I am thankful that I have had the honor to work with this talented individual.

I would also like to thank the folks at the First National Bank of Conway Springs, Kan., especially Bob Wall, a good friend and the bank president. Making this book into a reality required that others believe in the project. He did and I will always be grateful.

Some very talented Kansas writers also contributed to the essays in the book. My thanks to Cynthia Mines, Roberta Birk and Dorothy Belden for their time and effort spent on this project.

To my colleagues at KAKE, I cannot begin to thank all of you enough. Giving me the freedom to do this book has always been the hallmark of KAKE Television.

I'm proud of my Kansas heritage and hope that this book will change, in some way, the world's perception of our state.

These are not characters of Kansas – but Kansans of character.

Larry Hatteberg
November 1991
Wichita

Snapshot Biography

Larry Hatteberg was born June 30, 1944, in Winfield, and graduated from Winfield High School in 1962. He attended Emporia State University and Wichita State University. He married Judy Keller on June 6, 1965. They have two children, Sherry Renee and Susan Michele. Larry has worked at KAKE-TV in Wichita since 1963 and has been a news anchor since 1988. Years in Kansas: 47.

Butler County's Graveyard Reporter

Corrine Afton combines tombstone recording and genealogy to preserve history

When Corrine Afton was growing up, Decoration Day was a time when whole families gathered in cemeteries to decorate the graves of their dead.

"The cemetery is peaceful to me. A lot of people are uncomfortable in a cemetery, but I'm not. Maybe because I know this is where I'll end up one day."

The Benton grandmother is called "death's reporter" because of her cataloguing of gravestones. The memory of those lively family gatherings when she learned about her ancestors while helping to clean up and decorate their graves is one reason she is content to spend time in cemeteries today.

Cemeteries remind Corrine Afton of history, of generations past and of the nation she has grown to love more every year as she follows her avocation.

"To me the stones are first of all history, because there's data on there. There's artwork on them . . . The stones have a kind of personality."

She and her husband, John, work as a team, going up one row and down another, methodically recording data from tombstones. Many times they have to dig stones out of the ground, or scrub off moss and lichens that obscure the carving. They have completed 70 of the 72 cemeteries in Butler County, which has the largest land area of any Kansas county.

Butler County, which once covered territory to the Oklahoma line, was settled in 1857, four years before Kansas became a state. It has Civil War graves, and burials dating before the county's beginnings.

Once information is gathered from the stones, Corrine records it in her computer, which has a sorter that does cross-referencing. Using her computer, she has published seven alphabetized volumes of data from Butler County cemeteries, a boon for historians.

Corrine slipped naturally into her cemetery work. In 1976 the Aftons' first grandson was born, and she retired from her job as a school secretary so she could enjoy more time with the baby. The book *Roots* had just come out and the whole nation was newly interested in tracing families. And Corrine's mother had some genealogical information that was incomplete and needed to be compiled. She took on that task and is proud that within five years she has traced her mother's grandmother, long lost in family records, to a grave in Oregon.

Research in cemeteries led her to an interest in recording all the history, not just her own family's. In 1940 the Eula Houston Chapter of the Daughters of the American Revolution had copied stones in the western half of the county, but the rest was unrecorded. With the help of her husband, Corrine set to work. Her methodology includes sketching the sections in a graveyard and using a numbering system to record each stone. Her information is cross-referenced with the Eula Houston data.

Her work isn't confined to recording the cemeteries. She is certified by the National Genealogical Society, an all-important credential, and she often teaches seminars at Butler County Community College. Using her trusty computer, she has been working on a fund-raising project for the Butler County Historical Museum, transcribing the 1888 El Dorado City Directory, which has become faded and tattered over the years.

She and John spend their vacations searching out information in cemeteries all over the nation, and she is in demand to present her slide show, "My Favorite Rock Collection," which consists of pictures of interesting stones in Butler County.

Corrine says there are not enough hours in the day to get all her work done.

"I'll tell you, I won't be ready to go when my time comes," she says with a laugh.

She was born in Harper County, on the southern border of Kansas. Corrine spent her childhood there and in Grant County, Okla., where her grandparents lived.

In August 1944, her mother moved with her children to Wichita. Corrine graduated from Wichita High School East and then went to Washington, D.C., to work for the federal government—appropriately, in the Death Claims Department. She was there for about a year, the only time she'd lived outside Kansas. When she returned, she and John were married on Sept. 3, 1948. He is retired after 43 years with the Coleman Co. in Wichita.

Her family doesn't say much about her devotion to genealogy and cemeteries.

"I think my children's attitude is that it keeps Mom busy and keeps her from pestering us," she says with another laugh.

But when those children and grandchildren want to know about their roots, they can look to Corrine's research. She has fully documented "my four families" (grandparents on both sides) "and my husband's four families." She earns some money from her publication and other work, "just enough to support my expensive DAR habit." She is a member of the Isabella Weldin Chapter in Augusta.

The DAR, genealogy and cemeteries have nurtured her love of country. As she looks back on records of relatives who have fought and died for the United States, she has an ever greater feeling of patriotism.

Corrine is a woman with a cheerful outlook, a quick laugh and a way with words. She also is a woman who adheres to strict, old-fashioned values. And she is one who likes cemeteries.

"In the summer they are shady places; we love the birds, the plants and the trees."

And when it comes her time to lie in one:

"I hope when they walk by my stone in the Benton cemetery 50 years from now, they think, 'Oh, that's the lady who wrote all those books.' "

"To me the stones are first of all history . . ."

Snapshot Biography

Corrine Latta was born April 26, 1927, in Harper County. She married John Afton Sept. 3, 1948. They have three children: Alan, a university professor; Judi, a registered nurse; and Michael, who works for Boeing. She has five grandchildren. Years in Kansas: 63.

Urban Pioneers on Main Street

Gary and Patricia Anderson of Salina carve a niche downtown

Living on Main Street, above busy stores and occasionally noisy traffic, brings to mind much earlier days in this country's history or life in a city much larger than Salina. But Gary and Patricia Anderson have carved a very comfortable and luxurious home out of 5,600 square feet of upstairs building space in downtown Salina.

Work is just a few steps away at Vernon Jewelers, which Pat's family has owned since 1972. Gary and Pat both put in long days at the jewelry store. Gary works on watches and rings and precious jewels there.

"I like working with my hands. I feel like I do it well."

His main handiwork for the last few years, however, has been converting the upstairs space — which not long ago was full of pigeons, water damage and cracked walls — into a spacious living area that includes four bedrooms, three bathrooms, a pool room and bar, large living room and dining room, and a woodworking workshop. There may be no lawn for backyard barbecues, but Gary has cut a hole in the roof and he goes up there to cook on a grill. And there's no lawn to worry about mowing and no snow to shovel.

Pat got the idea to renovate the upstairs into living space a few months before she and Gary were married in 1988. They then set to work, armed with pencil, paper and plenty of dreams.

"I like unique surroundings to start with and the building itself was such a unique opportunity to do something that no one else had done. I couldn't resist it."

And the work took plenty of imagination. Constructed in the 1920s, the building housed an insurance company and various medical and law offices. It didn't exactly look like a home. But it does now.

"I didn't know if we could make this thing become a home out of being office space . . . . It's so big we thought we'd have to have intercoms, but we don't need that."

Their home is actually two buildings with a common stairway in between. It took a year to get it in livable condition, and even now, three years later, the work continues. The oak hardwood floors are

completed, the wallpaper is hung and the skylights let in plenty of sunshine, but Gary still has plans for those last two rooms: This winter, he'll be working on converting them into a gym and library.

Many people are surprised when they hear the Anderson's address, but many appreciate their attempt to keep downtown alive.

"At first they thought we were crazy. Now I think they're a little jealous," Gary said.

"Most people are really pleased that someone is doing something in the downtown area. There aren't many that have made the attempt to live in the downtown area."

They like the uniqueness of their downtown address.

"I'd much rather have this than a house that looks like everyone else's."

Gary figures the cost to create their home was less than if they'd bought and remodeled an existing home. In fact, an architect told him that if the work had been done professionally it would have cost $450,000.

"We could not build a house for this and have this kind of luxury."

And there's plenty of room for Gary's children, April, 11, and Chris, 9, and Pat's daughter, Kelli, 13.

Chris and April hone their bank shots as Gary and Pat survey their spacious home.

"They like it," Gary said. *"They're a little bit spoiled. Everybody has their own bedroom."*

It may have been Pat's dream to start with, but Gary has given the project his full attention for the last four years.

"This is really Pat's dream that has turned out to be my love. I can't describe it. It's something I felt like I wanted to do and it's turned into something great."

"We could not build a house for this and have this kind of luxury."

Clockwise: Gary, Pat, April, Kelli and Chris.

Snapshot Biography

Gary was born in Salina on Oct. 26, 1957, and Patricia was born in Goodland on July 1, 1953. He graduated from Salina South High School and she graduated from Dodge City High School. They were introduced by mutual friends and married in 1988 in Salina. They have three children: Kelli, 13; April, 11; and Chris, 9. Years in Kansas: Gary, 34; Pat, 38.

Small-Town Newspaper Editor
Les Anderson of Valley Center keeps the coverage consistent

The residents of Valley Center are Les Anderson's neighbors, friends and readers.

As founder and editor of the *Ark Valley News,* he's found that covering the big story in your hometown is sometimes tough.

"That's the difference between working at a big paper and a little paper — you can work at the (Wichita) Eagle and nobody knows who you are. In a small town, people you write about can be in your Sunday school class, buy gas where you do, go to PTA with you. . . . You get instant feedback. It's not always positive feedback but you know where you stand."

With help from a few friends and wife Nancy's retirement funds, they started the newspaper 16 years ago. Stories were banged out on a manual typewriter in a rented room ($60 a month included chair, desk and typewriter), pasted up in a friend's kitchen and the paper was personally thrown by the Andersons into every yard in Valley Center, a community of 4,000 just north of Wichita.

Word travels fast in small towns, but in this case the Andersons heard the encouraging words first-hand over coffee in the local cafe.

"They didn't know we were listening, it was neat to hear the reaction to what we'd done. It was the first time in a long time a lot of stuff had been covered on a regular basis."

But covering the news isn't always easy in a small town.

"I try to be fair and consistent. People have to respect that. They may not like it for a while. We've lost some friends over things we've done. But sometimes those are temporary losses."

Within the decade the paper would win some of the state's most coveted journalism awards. One of the biggest stories came in 1990 after a devastating windstorm swept through Valley Center.

"You have family and friends and when it's their houses and their belongings, it makes it tougher, a lot tougher."

Long nights are not unusual — while growing up the Anderson children spent much time in a nursery at the newspaper office — and putting out the paper following the storm was no exception.

"I wish we had more people and a little more time and I wish we hadn't been so tired when we put everything together. But I felt it was a pretty accurate reflection of what happened around here.

"The good thing about this is we had as much here as the Eagle or the radio/TV stations did. We were just as current and to me that's what it's all about."

After graduating from Valley Center High School — where he met his future wife and got his first taste of journalism in a senior class — Les earned a degree in English and journalism at Fort Hays State University. From there, he went to the University of Missouri, where he earned a master's in journalism in 1971. He got a job at the *Wichita Eagle* as copy editor and worked for both the *Eagle* and *Beacon* until 1974.

His journalism career then took him to the *Wichita Sun,* a weekly alternative newspaper he served as news editor. A year later he started the *Ark Valley News* in his hometown of Valley Center.

Nancy was still working full time as a nurse and Les was still at the *Sun* when they started the paper. At first it came out every two weeks but within a month it had become a weekly newspaper.

From May to September 1975 he competed with the *Valley Center Index.* When the Andersons bought the paper that fall, it had only 700 subscribers; they have boosted circulation to 2,100.

It was while Les was in graduate school that he first began to think about returning to his hometown to start a newspaper.

"When I was in Missouri, I thought about coming back and trying. It was something you think about, your hometown."

The newspaper office has moved four times, but always stayed within the same block on Valley Center's Main Street, where the barber, cafe owner and other merchants are not only neighbors but readers.

The newspaper ventures into waters not often charted by other small-town newspapers, such as endorsing candidates in local elections.

"We always have and we always will. We're more familiar with what's going on than the average person. Some papers even shy away from editorials, but that's one thing we've always done.

"We've had people cancel ads because they didn't like the way we did things."

Even in the best of times, it's difficult to make ends meet with just income from the newspaper, and Les is a partner in Valley Offset, a printing company, and a professor at Wichita State University.

And even in the most difficult of times, Les manages to keep his sense of humor. His friends can almost always count on Les to regale them with stories on small town Kansas life, university events or getting out the newspaper.

The *Ark Valley News* has given many WSU students their first taste of real-life journalism and teaching has given Les much satisfaction.

"It's kind of like being a little league coach when you see your kids go on and play major league sports, do a lot better than you did. You feel like you're doing some good."

He is just as pleased with awards his students or staff members win as with his own, which include the Victor Murdock Award for Excellence in Kansas Journalism.

Son Spike, who was only 4 when the venture started, now works part time at the newspaper in addition to majoring in sports business and communication at WSU. Nancy still fills most every production position, though she would someday like to return to nursing. The family of six grows its own vegetables and raises its own meat on 20 acres on the edge of town.

If Les could rewrite any of his own story, would he?

"No, I wouldn't change anything. I had chances to go to bigger papers, but that's not what I wanted to do. . . . For right now, I've got to decide what I'm going to do when I grow up, but I'm not sure I ever will."

Snapshot Biography

Les Anderson was born in Viola Nov. 23, 1948. He married his high school sweetheart, Nancy, in 1969 in Valley Center. He earned a bachelor's degree from Fort Hays State University in 1970 and a master's in journalism from the University of Missouri in 1971. They have four children: Matthew "Spike," Maggie, Ben and Seth. Years in Kansas: 42.

Creator of Special Greeting Cards

Judy Barnes of Winfield mixes love, imagination and acrylics

Judy Barnes blends her bent for philosophy and her love of painting to create one-of-a-kind greeting cards in a bright corner of her living room in Winfield.

"I make about 500 different styles, but if I had to choose, I would choose this one: 'All things are possible to him that believeth.' It's my favorite card because I believe it's the truth."

She started making the cards to provide meaningful greetings for family and friends. Messages, painted in colorful, flowing script, reflect Judy's personal philosophy.

Like her favorite, many messages are from the Bible, but she also borrows from Eastern religions, the Koran and from the philosophers she enjoys reading in her spare time. All the messages reflect her own beliefs.

"I hope the cards help people think about looking within themselves for enrichment, purpose and joy in life, rather than looking outward for happiness or fulfillment." Another message from her heart: "By believing in one's self, one can accomplish anything."

But the cards are more than messages. They are colorful, textured works of art, made with thick application of acrylic paint or watercolor marker pens in a style she calls primitive. Each card is created individually, with disciplined spontaneity.

Judy's career toward becoming a creator of special cards evolved slowly.

Though she has lived in Winfield since 1967, when her husband began teaching at Southwestern College, it wasn't until she joined an art group later that her "dabbling" with cards began.

In 1979, when Dick took a job in Dallas, she began pursuing the card business intensively. She soon was marketing the greetings, which were popular almost immediately. The commercial interest continued after they returned to Winfield.

"I began painting as just a hobby or just something to pass the time. When you're in that field you can express the deepest and clearest emotion, I think."

That doesn't mean she landed in an easy dreamworld career. An extensive marketing effort was necessary to achieve and maintain her success, and it takes discipline to turn out the cards. Some weeks she doesn't work at all; others, she paints the greetings all day several days in a row. Her busiest time is October through the middle of May, which encompasses the holidays — Christmas, Valentine's Day and Mother's Day — when her cards are in greatest demand.

"I make up orders as they come in. I like to send them out fresh, like freshly baked cookies."

The cards go to representatives in New York, on the West Coast and in Dallas who place them in shops in 12 to 13 states. Although they cost $5 each, the attractive cards sell readily and steadily.

She is comfortable with the relatively easy pace of the business and is not sure she wants to see it stepped up.

"I like it the way it is now. I can do exactly what I want, say what I want and be in total control. The cards are a statement of my philosophy and beliefs. I don't want to compromise that." Besides, "I make an adequate income."

A personalized greeting card made like a freshly baked cookie.

Gradually she has increased the time devoted to another endeavor: painting larger artworks that are sold privately to collectors.

In her spare time, Judy likes to take walks and study or just read philosophers such as Plato and other Greeks and a smattering of contemporary thinkers.

The family recently moved from a larger house to a cottage. Designed by a local architect, William Caton, it is made of "beautiful wood, brick and Silverdale stone" and Judy , the artist, almost croons over its loveliness. The living room has a whole wall of windows, making Judy's working corner "a studio in every sense of the word."

One message that she doesn't paint is, nevertheless, part of her philosophy.

"Profit is the least of my concerns. My greatest concern, I think, is to communicate beauty, love, joy, the beautifulness of life. I don't think you can create anything without having a part of yourself in that creation. It is an expression of love."

Snapshot Biography

Judy Barnes was born Dec. 2, 1938, in Dallas, Texas, where she met her future husband while in high school. They were married in 1958 and have a son, John, 31, and a daughter, Jennifer, 22. She attended Southern Methodist University and the University of Texas-Austin. Years in Kansas:19.

Goessel's Exotic Animal Lovers

On Vernon and Angela Base's farm, buffalo roam free in menagerie

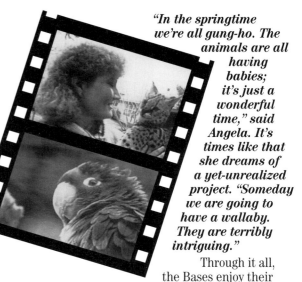

On Vernon and Angela Base's farm, two and a half acres near the town of Goessel, there is much more than a moo-moo here and a neigh-neigh there.

Exotic birds chirp, chatter and sing in the old house and in cages in the yard. Goats, cats, dogs and deer roam the barnyard. A well-fed tawny cougar snarls a greeting from her quarters. In adjacent rented pastureland, horses and buffalo roam free. There are three rabbits, deer, an African bush cat. Those are only some of the animals that keep the whole family working hard on this miniature sanctuary. Always, however, they count the blessings of living with their demanding, amusing, beautiful and interesting menagerie.

"I couldn't imagine giving this up," said Angela. "We may not have money in the checkbook but wealth is just abounding around us in the way of wildlife."

Both the Bases are 34, born six months apart. Angela grew up in the house the family now occupies. Vernon's childhood home is only a couple of miles away.

Their children, Joe and Lacie, go to school in Goessel, just as their parents did, and they have had some of the same teachers who taught Vernon and Angela.

Their collection of animals also is a continuation of childhood experiences. Vernon and Angela grew up with the usual farm animals. After they married in 1977 they had horses, beef cattle, dogs and cats. Then about eight years ago they attended a sale of buffalo at the nearby Maxwell Game Preserve and came home with a few of the shaggy beasts. They liked the semi-wildness of the animals, and when the buffalo and cattle proved incompatible, the cattle were sold.

They have a Kansas breeders license so they can buy, breed and sell exotic animals, and they are in close touch with other breeders throughout the region. Sometimes people ask them to take animals. Their very old mare came in trade for a yellow and gray cockatiel.

One animal often leads to another. For example, when the cougar, Tisha, had her first litter, the Bases learned that formula for baby cougars was expensive. Goat milk is a good substitute, so they bought the

pygmy and Nubian goats, which keep them well supplied. Now they even sell some milk to other breeders. The pygmy goats, which the Bases are breeding to even-smaller size, are the stars of any festival where they are exhibited. One little goat regularly performs a spontaneous dance atop a feedbox, to the delight of family and visitors.

About four years ago Angela decided to breed birds for sale and trade. Earlier in 1991 her flock included cockatiels, love birds, orange-winged Amazon parrots, cockatoo and others from around the world. But she grew tired of the noisy aviary and the unceasing demands for hand-feeding, so she's been phasing out the birds, intending to keep only a few favorites.

The small farm's large population of living creatures attracts many visitors, especially during the school year. In 1990-91, five school districts brought grade-school pupils out to see the Base animals. Originally there was no charge, but now the Bases ask 50 cents from each child to compensate for their time.

Both Vernon and Angela have jobs. He is a full-time welder at Excel, a manufacturer in nearby Hesston, and she is a part-time clerk at a store near their home. They dream of the day they can quit their jobs and devote all their time to their animals.

"This is our investment," said Vernon. Angela chimed in, "We're supporting them. Someday I'd like all this to support us."

The two children help with the chores.

"Sure, they get tired of it, sometimes, just like I get tired. But they have exposure to the animals, and experiences other kids don't have," said Vernon.

Some friends and relatives look askance at the Bases' venture, but others approve and stand ready to help when needed.

There are discouraging times, such as when the fox terrier destroyed the lily pond, or the early days when illness struck frequently. But these days the Bases are experienced enough that their animals rarely get sick, and there is a peacefulness about their farm that makes up for headaches.

The best time is spring.

"In the springtime we're all gung-ho. The animals are all having babies; it's just a wonderful time," said Angela. It's times like that she dreams of a yet-unrealized project. "Someday we are going to have a wallaby. They are terribly intriguing."

Through it all, the Bases enjoy their life and they continually grow in their admiration of animals.

"The very fact of their survival in the wild is awesome," Angela said. "I hear people talk about dumb animals. They're not dumb. They're smart and they're terribly interesting."

Lacie Base, 6, plays with a wooly friend at her family's farm.

Vernon Base pets the family cougar as Angela and children Joe and Lacie watch.

Snapshot Biography

Vernon Base was born Dec. 24, 1956, and Angela was born June 9, 1957. They graduated from Goessel High School and were married in 1977. They have two children: Joe, 12, and Lacie, 6. Years in Kansas: 34.

Marion's Old-Fashioned Grocers

You can charge and get delivery at Jack and Vernie Beaston's store

Jack delivers groceries in his pick-up.

As we get older, life sometimes seems to get a little too complicated. That's why it's nice to find those little places tucked away in small towns that have been etched in your memory since childhood.

Such a place is in Marion, at the Beaston Market. It's the kind of business the rest of us dream about. Vernie and Jack Beaston are their own bosses, and Jack doesn't believe he would want it any other way.

"As many years as I've worked for myself, I don't think I could work for anybody else."

Vernie still takes grocery orders over the phone, writes the list on an old-fashioned order pad and records the amounts on bills for the customers who charge their groceries. Others shop in person. The bookkeeping system needs no computer.

"We just have our little sales book and they get their cart and come up and fill it up and we write down each item and the price and say good-bye. Each customer has their own little stall of sales slips and we keep it posted every day and at the end of the month they come in and pay."

The Beaston Market is one of the few that still delivers. They don't just have customers, they have friends. Jack talked about the differences as he drove a small pickup filled with groceries to houses around Marion.

"This one lady I just delivered to, she has a fixed schedule and if I don't hear from her, I call her just to make sure she's all right."

Jack and Vernie don't believe they are unusual; they say they are traditional small-town merchants. Their friends say differently.

"They are not only good friends, they're good merchants."

The Beastons are running the store just as Jack's father and grandfather did before them. Jack cannot remember a time when the store, noted for its high ceilings and wooden-floors, was not a part of his life.

"I've probably been around the store since I was big enough to talk. When I was a kid, I remember sleeping under the bread racks."

The store has begun to attract sightseers, even from out-of-state, since the spring of 1991 when it was featured on KAKE-TV. One visitor yearned to see the string, hanging from the ceiling, that once was used to wrap freshly cut meat.

"I said, no, we'd graduated to Scotch tape."

The meat, though, still is cut to order, using Jack's experienced eye to gauge the weight before the cut is made.

"I've been at it long enough to know about what it weighs."

The Beastons expect the tradition to end about 1994, when they plan to retire. The store, which is open six days a week from 8 a.m. to 6 p.m., probably will be closed. And the couple, who often spend part of Sundays taking care of other store-related business, will be able to spend more time relaxing and expanding their activities with the Valley Methodist Church. Jack speculated on the future.

"I think we're probably one of the last. I don't think it'll go on anymore. I always thought if you had a business of your own, it would be pretty stable, but there are so many benefits you lose. I can't see anybody buying it. We'll just have to close it . . . . I think the tradition is ending right now."

"We just have our little sales book and they get their cart and come up and fill it up and we write down each item and the price and say good-bye. Each customer has their own little stall of sales slips and we keep it posted every day and at the end of the month they come in and pay."

The Beastons with customers Debbie Darrow and daughter Carrie: "They give credit so young families can eat."

SNAPSHOT BIOGRAPHY

Jack Beaston was born April 6, 1919. Vernie was born June 20, 1928. They both graduated from Marion High School and attended Emporia State University, where Jack earned a bachelor's degree in business administration. They have a daughter, Martha Kae Heigert, a son, Brook Jae Beaston, and one grandchild. Years in Kansas: all their lives.

The First Lady of Aviation

Olive Ann Beech busy in retirement, after six decades with 'family' firm

In 1940, as the United States and Beech Aircraft Co. prepared for the possibility of war, Walter H. Beech became ill. Olive Ann Beech, then 38, stepped forward to take on the leadership of the company.

"When we entered into the war production, that took all your time and effort to make things run smoothly. Of course, everything didn't always run smoothly, as we grew from 700 people to a couple of thousand. But it still felt like we were a small family."

It was boom time in Wichita. Plants were operating around the clock. Wichitans made the planes that helped win the war.

The company geared up for defense production as the demand for military versions of the Beechcraft Models 17 and 18 pushed backlogs from $22 million in 1940 to $82 million the next year. Employment quadrupled in three years to more than 4,000.

One of Mrs. Beech's first actions was to arrange for a $50 million loan from a syndicate of 36 banking firms to finance the military production.

"That was just potato chips."

Wheeling and dealing in the world of finance was not foreign to Olive Ann Beech. She had a bank account at the age of 7, and at 11 was given the responsibility of paying the family bills.

In 1917, Olive Ann Mellor's family had moved from Paola to Wichita, where she attended business college. Later,

she joined the Travel Air Manufacturing Co. as secretary and bookkeeper. Its principal was Walter H. Beech, a former World War I pilot. Travel Air became the world's leading producer of commercial airplanes in the 1920s.

In 1929, Mr. Beech merged Travel Air with Curtiss Wright, and the next year Walter and Olive Ann were married. They lived in New York City for two years, then returned to Wichita to found Beech Aircraft Co.

In the first year, not a single airplane was sold, but the next year saw the sale of the first Beechcraft, a classic Model 17 single-engine Staggerwing biplane.

Her influence as secretary-treasurer on the company was not limited to finance. In 1936 she convinced her husband to let Louise Thaden and Blanche Noyes fly a Beechcraft Model 17 in the Bendix Transcontinental Speed Dash, reasoning that a win by a woman pilot would be more impressive. And Thaden and Noyes lived up to their end of the bargain, piloting the plane to victory.

Mrs. Beech began learning the nuts and bolts of the business by carefully studying a complete breakdown drawing of an airplane after being teased about her misuse of aircraft terms. However, she never learned to fly.

"The pilots used to want to teach me to fly. But their idea of teaching me was going through all the stunts they knew how to do, so that cooled me down."

In 1941 Mr. Beech's health improved and he returned to Beech. The two guided the company as it made a major contribution to the war effort.

During the war, Beech Aircraft employment reached a peak of 14,000, producing 7,400 military Beechcrafts.

The company's momentum continued after the war, as the Beechcraft Model D18S was the first post-war airplane to be certified. That was followed by the V-tail Beechcraft Bonanza in 1946 and the twin-Bonanza in 1949.

The next year brought the Korean War and sudden tragedy to the Beech family when Walter Beech died of a heart attack. Mrs. Beech was elected president and chairman of the board at the age of 47.

Although she had become the nation's only female chief executive of a major aircraft company, Olive Ann Beech never gave much thought to being a woman in a man's world.

"No I didn't, because I always worked with men. But you know we always treated our people as individuals, whether they were man or woman. If they couldn't do the job, that was too bad."

To meet Korean War defense demands, the Beech payroll jumped from $2,500 to more than $13,000.

Mrs. Beech assembled an executive team of people "who liked to find ways to do things, not tell me why they can't be done." The team clicked and Beech was hugely successful.

In the 1950s, the King Air was introduced. Beginning in the 1960s, the company's research led to Beechcraft products playing a role in the nation's space efforts, including the Gemini, Apollo, Lunar and space shuttle programs.

In 1968, Mrs. Beech turned over the presidency to Frank Hedrick, and the two guided the company through its delivery of the 40,000th Beechcraft in 1977.

Beech sales tripled to $719 million between 1973 and 1980. That same year, following the merger of Beech with Raytheon, Mrs. Beech was elected to Raytheon's board of directors, and she received two of aviation's most distinguished honors: the "Sands of Time" Kitty Hawk Civilian Award and the Wright Brothers Memorial Trophy. In 1981, she was named to the Aviation Hall of Fame. The next year, she retired as Beech's chairman, but continues to serve as chairman emeritus.

Today, at 88, Olive Ann Beech still leads a busy life. She is active as a philanthropist and patron of the arts, religion and education. She still pays the bills as she did at the age of 11, enjoys writing, attending lunches and keeping up with her grandchildren .

When the family and grandchildren are around, "We like to kid a lot, and I collect pigs, the porcelain kind.

"I reserve the right to do what I want to do each day," Mrs. Beech said of her retirement lifestyle. *"I don't enjoy being in the public eye, though I suppose I had my share of it."*

As the First Lady of Aviation, she most certainly did.

Snapshot Biography:

Olive Ann Mellor was born Sept. 25, 1903, in Waverly. She attended school in Paola and business college in Wichita. She married Walter H. Beech on Feb. 24, 1930. She has two children, Mrs. Suzanne Warner, California, and Mrs. Mary Lynn Oliver, Wichita; and three grandchildren. Years in Kansas: 86.

Wichita's Colorful Newspaper Columnist
Bonnie Bing's light shines in more than just fashion and society worlds

One of the first impressions you get in meeting *Wichita Eagle* columnist Bonnie Bing is that she bubbles like new champagne. She has the perfect personality for her job — enthusiasm and a warm and restless spirit.

At a fashion shoot, she's the cheerleader:

"This is going to be great. This is going to be a great shot . . . we have to fool mother nature."

But there is no fooling Bonnie Bing. Everything has to be perfect for her fall fashion shoot. She controls everything but the weather.

"We've got to hurry, it's not raining right now. They're so skinny the raindrops go on either side of them anyway."

People who don't know Bonnie Bing believe her job entails writing a little column for the paper then dashing off for some quiche. But some fashion shoots turn out to be 17-hour days.

"It's lots of hard work . . . and if my energy level goes down, I've noticed the models' energy level goes down. When you model, if you have a pretty face that's not enough, your energy has to come from within. It's hard work.

"I think what I don't have in talent, I make up for in energy . . . which is pretty scary when you get old."

At a fashion shoot, Bonnie — often the only one not dressed up — directs with a passion, and with a glow in her eye like a kid in a candy store.

"I have a sickness for clothes. I love clothes. A really beautiful piece of clothing, well tailored out of wonderful fabric is like a piece of art I think . . . beautiful.

"People say it will take two years for that style to get to Wichita, that is simply not true. It doesn't take any longer to get here than it does anywhere else. If they don't see it here, it's because we choose not to buy it and not to wear it."

Bonnie is also the society columnist. Let's face it, many of us view the society column as just written about the rich folks in town. Bonnie says no way.

"It's not a society-snooty thing. It's a column that tells what's happening in Wichita . . . and the more parts of town I hear from the better I like it."

Bonnie took a circuitous route to end up as a newspaper columnist. A native Wichitan and Wichita State University graduate, she was a junior high teacher before becoming assistant athletic director for women's programs at WSU. One of her specialties was fund raising.

Eagle Editor Davis "Buzz" Merritt and an assistant recruited Bonnie to write the society column.

"I knew a lot of people and I knew that I could talk. I just didn't know if I could write."

After some hesitation, she took the job, and friends at the paper coached her in her writing. It's important to Bonnie that there is more to her job than writing the society "Happenings" and fashion "Remnant" columns, though she is quick to point out: "Going to Dallas and New York is still thrilling."

What she really enjoys is the variety of her job.

"I enjoy writing features. Whether I'm meeting the San Diego Chicken, riding an elephant, being in a milking contest at the State Fair, or meeting Dixie Carter of 'Designing Women,' I never know each week what I'm going to do. I really like that."

Bonnie's red hair and natural humor have also lit up the stage for Gridiron productions, a satirical review of state and local politics produced and directed by local journalists. She doesn't have to try very

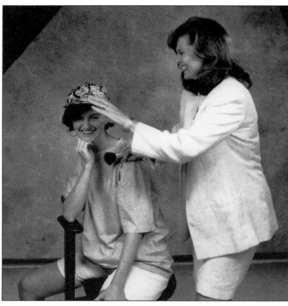

Bonnie Bing puts finishing touches on model Angie Reiff before a shoot at the Eagle.

hard to be a ham. But there is a serious side to this ball of energy.

She's on the boards of the YWCA, the WSU Alumni Association, the Wichita Historical Museum, and volunteers for a number of other organizations.

Yet what really gets her talking is the Roots and Wings organization. Bonnie serves as a Court Appointed Special Advocate (CASA) for children in dire straits. Her job is to see actions are taken to provide for the child's legal, physical and emotional needs.

"These are kids that have slipped through the cracks. They're dirt poor. It makes you appreciate what you have in life."

Often, these are kids whose families are going through tremendous turmoil.

"It's important to be there for them each week. Once they understand you are there just for them, they'll tell you things they won't tell anybody else."

Whether it's mixing in the world of fashion or society, milking a cow or riding an elephant, attending a board meeting or hanging out with one of her "kids" from Roots and Wings, there are two ingredients Bonnie Bing brings to all these activities — a spirited enthusiasm and a giant smile.

Snapshot Biography

Bonnie Bing was born April 15, 1947, in Wichita. She graduated from Wichita North, then graduated from WSU in 1969, majoring in education. She obtained a master's in education and taught six years at Pleasant Valley Junior High before joining the WSU Athletic Department. She has been married to attorney Dick Honeyman for six years. Years in Kansas: 44.

The Keeper of the Animals

Ron Blakely knew before kindergarten he would be a zookeeper

Ron Blakely got into zoo work because he loves animals. He got out of it, taking early retirement March 1, 1991, as director of the Sedgwick County Zoo, for the same reason.

"I was spending most of my time dealing with people and agencies, and getting further and further away from animals."

Blakely knew even before he entered kindergarten that he wanted to be a zookeeper. By 1991, he had worked 45 years in zoos, and was the longest-term practicing zoo worker in the American Association of Zoological Parks and Aquariums.

He has a deep respect for all animals.

"Unlike some people, I know animals can think. I've been out-thought too many times by them."

He came to Wichita from Chicago, where he worked for six years at the Lincoln Park Zoo and Brookfield Zoo. In less than 24 years, working with volunteers, government officials and staff, he built the Sedgwick County Zoo into one of the premier educational zoos in the world, with six major exhibit areas and a North American Prairie exhibit under construction.

His first task in Sedgwick County was to survey, from an airplane, land that the Zoological Society proposed to buy. He approved and the zoo soon started

Retired zoo director Ron Blakely now spends his days on 80 acres near Cheney with his dog, cat and a few miniature horses.

taking form. It grew to encompass nearly 1,500 animals on 212 acres in northwest Wichita and a 40-acre breeding farm near Hutchinson.

Once retired, however, Blakely left all that behind to live with his cat, dog and a few miniature horses on 80 acres on the Ninnescah River near Cheney.

His new activities involve new dreams relating to animals, plants and people. His biggest project is to start raising minor breeds of domestic animals.

"They are old rare breeds of domestic animals, many of which are in danger of extinction. Once they are gone they cannot be recreated."

Blakely is chairman of the board of American Minor Breeds Conservancy, which is dedicated to bringing back old breeds. When Blakely sells his land and buys 160 acres elsewhere, he wants to start breeding such animals as White Galloway beef cattle.

Among his many projects is working with a Wichita production company to create a television series in which he will appear as "The Neighborhood Naturalist." The programs, each two minutes long, deal with plants and animals and their relationships with people.

Out of a spare bedroom Blakely does all the work related to two major posts among his peers. In addition to chairing the Minor Breeds Conservancy, he is chairman of the International Society of Zooculturists

Blakely grew up with parents who went to great lengths to nurture his love of animals. For 14 years he had a Japanese Silky rooster that lived outdoors in summer and spent the winters in the basement.

"One time my parents went away and I slept in their bed. At dawn, that rooster was crowing right under their room. They had put up with that all those years and never said a word."

Constant reading and working with animals made Blakely knowledgeable at an early age. At 17 he carried a locker full of snakes around to schools in the Southeast, and gave lectures in five schools each day, under auspices of the U.S. Society of Zoology. In summers, he worked with an animal show at a carnival. At 18 he had a three-lion animal act.

"Back when I knew everything, I knew I did not need to go to college to study ethology."

Then he visited Dr. William Mann, director of the National Zoo in Washington. A leading figure among zoologists, Mann asked the youngster when he was going to college. "I'm not," Blakely replied, to which Dr. Mann responded, "Oh, yes you are. As of now, I am blackballing you in the profession until you get your degree."

Four years later Blakely had the degree from Michigan State. He then visited Dr. Mann again, who pointed him toward a job with the Columbus Zoo, in the giraffe house. Later, ready to make a change, Blakely placed an ad: "College graduate familiar with use of broom and shovel desires zoo position."

Marlin Perkins, director of the Lincoln Park Zoo in Chicago who was known to television viewers for his forays into the wild, hired Blakely. For six years the young man was curator of birds. Then he spent six years as director of the Brookfield Zoo.

One thing that has not changed throughout his career is his philosophy:

"The joy of being alive is being alive in a community of living things, not being alive by yourself. Plants, animals, the climate — everything is interrelated. There is just no end to it.

On his last day at the Sedgwick County Zoo, Blakely bid farewell to many animal friends, including Charlie, his long time monkey pal.

"The joy of being alive is being alive in a community of living things . . . ."

Snapshot Biography

Ron Blakely was born Nov. 29, 1931, in Detroit and grew up in Lansing, Mich. He graduated from Michigan State University earning degrees in psychology and zoology. He became director of the new Sedgwick County Zoo in 1967; a few months after his retirement in 1991, the zoo dedicated the R.L. Blakely Center. Years in Kansas: 24.

Conserver of Missouri River Life

Wolf River Bob Breeze traded Hollywood for White Cloud countryside

White Cloud, Kansas. Where the Missouri River meets the Nebraska border, and time ambles by like an old dog full of the afternoon sun.

Wolf River Bob knows this country well. Bob Breeze — for that is his name, though it seldom is used — is a student of nature and a teacher of life.

"A person that knows history looks back into the past so he can look ahead more intelligently."

Wolf River Bob does just that. He sees the countryside as the explorers Lewis and Clark did when they trekked through the White Cloud area in 1804 and he plans to preserve his corner of Kansas for future generations.

"I help nature. Nature does a hell of a job for me. Then I have got all the help with me every day. I have Father Time, Mother Nature. They all help me with this project. They plant

Wolf River Bob (on horse) worked in Hollywood with Ray Crash Corrigan, one of the Three Musketeers.

the trees for me and they come up on their own. I clean it up and make it nice."

His instincts for conservation mesh well with his instincts for promoting White Cloud to tourists. He explained how he manages that balance as he gazed across the valley below Lewis and Clark Lookout on his property.

"Right now I can think, by looking down here, I can see Lewis and Clark coming up that river with their keel boats and everything — mountain men who didn't know anything about this area, that's why I stress to anybody who comes to visit, please leave nothing but happy tracks and take nothing but pictures. And then you're welcome back."

Wolf River Bob himself was welcomed back to White Cloud by its citizens after 25 years of putting on western shows and performing as a stuntman in Hollywood.

It was in Hollywood that Wolf River Bob acquired his nick name – when friends suggested he needed a "crazy" stage name. Wolf River is nine miles south of White Cloud. Bob's film and television career included working with Roy Rogers and Hoot Gibson, and appearances in several "Wagon Train" episodes.

Despite all the glamour and the lights, Bob Breeze found himself with an empty feeling after two decades in Hollywood. What he missed was Kansas.

"If I had this in California, I could settle back and be a billionaire because this view right here, Los Angeles would give a billion dollars for. But I wouldn't want it out there 'cause they would pollute it and you couldn't see across the river."

Now — in large part because of his efforts — thousands of people are coming to White Cloud and looking across that same Missouri River. Wolf River Bob started a flea market and country show to bring people to town after he returned from Hollywood. The money earned was used to support the local historical society. The event brings in about 25,000 people twice each year.

He is putting up a building and an arena for bigger, better country-western shows and horse shows, and he dreams of turning part of his property into a place for trail rides. Already, people come in for "primitive" camping and lessons about nature. He also

Wolf River Bob cracks the whip.

brings in Indian shows from the Iowa Sac and Fox reservation about nine miles away at Highland. Tourists from other states and foreign countries seem to have discovered White Cloud, and the White Cloud residents finally are taking pride in what nature has given them.

"It took 'em several years to wise up to the fact that this area's beautiful. They don't have to go to Colorado or the Ozarks. It's interesting. I love it. I'm living the good life."

*"It took 'em
several years
to wise up to
the fact that this
area's beautiful."*

Snapshot Biography

Wolf River Bob was born Bob Breeze on Dec. 10, 1926, in
White Cloud, where he attended school. He has one son,
Raymond. Years in Kansas: 40.

Ark City's Old-Time Hardware Merchant
Alan Bryant's store offers charm, computers and hog tongs

Something old, something new. There is plenty of both in Bryant Hardware in Arkansas City, but for most customers the charm is in the old.

Old barnwood walls, pressed tin ceilings, antique equipment such as the hand-cranked cash register capture attention in the hardware store owned and operated by two brothers and their wives, Alan and Kathy Bryant and John and Christie Bryant. They have another old-fashioned advantage: service.

"We have a lot of do-it-yourself business," said Alan, their spokesman, in his slow, soft drawl. "If a little widow comes in, we'll probably fix it for her."

The brothers and their employees will work with the amateurs, helping them know just what tool or gadget is needed and how to do the job. John even stops by the home of one handicapped customer and friend to change his light bulbs.

"In a little town, you take care of each other. There is a lot of reward in working with people."

But the store is more than a quaint anachronism. It has a full line of hardware. Computers have replaced the old "want book" for inventory, ordering merchandise and keeping books. In an adjoining building is Bryant Collectibles, a gift shop established 15 years ago to reach out to newlyweds and other customers not turned on by hardware.

"Our mother really loves gift shops, and I guess that's why I started it. I started it in a corner of the store and kept expanding."

The hardware store had its beginnings in

1870, in a building at 106 S. Summit, a couple of doors away from the present site. Their grandfather, Lew Bryant, bookkeeper for a wholesale hardware business in Wichita, bought into it in 1926, using the equity in the family home. He was manager, and gradually bought out the backers.

"Grandpa and Grandma practically lived at the store," Alan said. "I can't really imagine building a business while going through the Depression."

When the present owners' father, Victor, came back from World War II, he took over the business and operated it with his wife, Dorothy. Now retired to Scottsdale, Ariz., they still own the buildings but Alan and John took over the stock and equipment.

Alan, a "war baby" born Dec. 28, 1944, took his place in the business full time in 1966 after graduating from the University of Kansas. John, born Sept. 27, 1952, came into the store in the early '70s, after college. Besides the brothers, there are four sisters.

"We all went to KU except for one sister who snuck off to K-State," Alan chuckled.

John and Alan grew up helping in the store, but the hardware business has changed. There used to be an in-house plumber, but he left. At one time a lot of sales representatives called to take orders.

"But now John has that computer thing he puts on the telephone and it can handle thousands of items."

The community has changed, too. Once farmers were the big customers, but as farming has declined, industry has increased, and it has brought in lots of employees from as far away as New York, Canada and Australia. Occasionally, people who have left Kansas have dropped in while on nostalgic visits.

"They will say, 'I never realized what a unique little store this is' until they went looking for hardware items in another city."

Alan is the collector who is responsible for much of the old equipment he's found and installed, and the old tools, including a hog tong, hanging on the walls. Merchandise includes hog rings and even flypaper. Small items are kept handy in old wooden bins or cut-off cardboard boxes.

Alan Bryant helps Roger Brown, president of Home National Bank and a long-time friend and customer, find an item at the hardware store.

"We do have an old look; there are lots of things you can't find anywhere else."

Collecting also is a personal hobby for Alan, and besides finding the items, he likes to research the history connected with them. An "old gentleman" long ago got him interested in pocket knives, and he has a good collection of them. He also collects duck decoys, fishing tackle and tools. He has turned his teenage son, Matthew, into a collector, too, who often goes to flea markets searching for straight razors and duck decoys.

In every sense, the hardware store and gift shop are a family business. Christie, who is working on her college degree, works part time in the gift shop. Kathy teaches high school English full time so is not so involved. Alan and Kathy have three children: Leanne and Allison, who are KU students, and Matthew, a high school junior. All three work or have worked in the business. John's sons, Zachary and Andrew, both in grade school, have started coming in to sweep.

"Trying to make it today is pretty tough. You have a lot of competition. Government people are always coming around to check on pesticides, check our scales or to be sure we have the right permit to sell grass and garden seeds. There are lots of regulations. We have to wear a lot of hats and sometimes they're coming at us from many directions. But this store is something to be proud of."

n Bryant assists Mable Kitchens while Alan proudly displays the antique cash register.

Snapshot Biography

Alan Bryant was born Dec. 28, 1944, in Battle Creek, Mich., where his father was in the military service. He attended Arkansas City schools and the University of Kansas. He married Kathy, who also grew up in Arkansas City, Aug. 5, 1967; they have three children. Years in Kansas: 46.

The Clarion's Cub Reporter
Erin Caffrey of Mount Hope not afraid to be nosy with dignitaries

It takes guts to be a newspaper reporter, says Erin Caffrey, 13, who has been writing a column for the *Mount Hope Clarion* for four years. It took some courage for a 9-year-old to approach the paper about writing a column.

"I saw 'Reading Rainbow' on television. They reviewed children's books and I thought I could do that."

She not only was able to do the reviews, but the *Clarion* soon promoted her to about-town reporting, pleasant little features about such events as a new little park made by the bank or getting ready for Christmas.

A sample from 1989: "Mr. and Mrs. Harris had the best steps to sit on and visit. They have the best popcorn balls in the whole world.

"Last week when it was cold, Les Dick let his three ducks into the shed so they could stay warm. To thank him, they left a big mess for him to clean."

She still does chatty reporting but she has graduated to gutsy reporting and commentary. In August of 1991, shortly before she started the eighth grade, she came within an inch of losing her job because she wrote a column critical of the scheduling of junior high music and physical education classes.

"We have only 20 minutes for music and 20 minutes for PE," she said indignantly. "In PE, we don't even have time to change clothes. And in music, it takes us five minutes to get going. That leaves us only 15 minutes."

That is not enough, in the opinion of the five-foot blonde who sings alto in school musical groups, and who is the only percussionist in the junior high band. When the column came out, the community of 800 was divided. Many complimented her on tackling the subject and on writing well. Others were not amused. Among the latter was her publisher, Bill Chance, who was on the school board when it adopted the music-PE schedule.

"He kind of blew his top and was going to fire me. But he checked all of it out and found out the information was accurate."

So Erin still is writing her column. But she's learned that writing about something doesn't necessarily change it. The 20-minute classes prevailed in the fall term.

She also refused to abide by the rules when she covered the inauguration of Gov. Joan Finney in January 1991. At noon, the governor retired to eat lunch and the press was ordered to stay out. Erin went right in and was in the room a few minutes before the governor's staff spotted her camera and press pass and hustled her away. She reported that Mrs. Finney had dined on a sandwich and potato chips.

"It just takes guts," she said. "And you have to be nosy."

Among other favorite stories she's covered is the visit of an agricultural delegation from the Soviet Union to a farm near Haven. The chairman of the delegation gave the young reporter a hug and a kiss. She also covered President George Bush's visit to Kansas, but got neither hug nor kiss.

Erin writes about a quarter of a page a week. She rarely misses a deadline, usually only when she is out of town on vacation. Penalty for missed deadlines is simple. She doesn't get published that week. And she likes seeing her words in print.

"The paper goes all over the country, and I hear from lots of people. My great aunt in California reads the paper; she says I should keep on writing."

Erin used to say she wanted to study journalism when she went to college. Now she is not sure. She enjoys music, including beating all kinds of drums, and vocalizing with school and church groups as well as in vaudeville, talent shows and Christian concerts. Her favorites are "wacky" songs like "Second-Hand Rose." She also enjoys acting. She may, she said, want to study music or drama when she enrolls at the University of Kansas in a few years.

Meanwhile, her $25-a-month salary goes into saving for a computer. Her editor, Delores Weve, admires Erin's rapport with older people, as well as friends her age.

This is her last year of classes in Mount Hope. In 1992, she will be bused to Haven to enter high school, and she's having the usual eighth-grade trepidations.

"It's bigger; they have about 125 students; it's kind of scary to think about."

But once she gets her pen and notepad in hand, it's not likely Erin Caffrey will be afraid to ask questions.

Erin interviews her uncle, Richard Caffrey, for an article about harvest.

Snapshot Biography

Erin Caffrey was born in Newton on May 30, 1978, but has spent her life in Mount Hope, reared by her mother's parents, Paul and Mary Ann Caffrey. Her mother and stepfather, Barbara and Timothy Hatch, live in Wichita. She dotes on her two little sisters: Ashley, born Jan. 10, 1990, and Breana, born Jan. 30, 1991. Years in Kansas: 13.

Egg Painter Polishes Ukrainian Art

Wichita's Marilyn Cain uses wax and dye to produce intricately decorated eggs

Don't ask Marilyn Cain of Wichita how she "paints" the vivid Ukrainian eggs she creates and sells by the dozen.

"I don't use paint or a paint brush. I use wax and dye, just the way a child would make an Easter egg by writing his name in wax, then dipping it in dye. The dye covers all of the egg except for the writing, so when it is finished, the name stands out in the natural color of the egg."

Marilyn's work, of course, is infinitely more complex. A big lighted cabinet in the Cain living room is filled with eggs, in bright colors and complex patterns. Some she has collected, some she created in her upstairs workroom, using the stylus and wax to "write" them in the traditional way, using traditional Ukrainian patterns that she combines in her own way. A typewritten glossary, which she gives to those who buy her eggs, explains the meanings of the hieroglyphs and colors, as she learned them.

"The egg itself is an icon of the universe. If it is not balanced, it is believed it will topple over, so the pattern and color must be the same on both sides."

The patterns are rich in Christian symbolism. For example, a star or a rose is an ancient symbol of Christ and heralds Christ's birth. They also symbolize God's love toward men. A triangle stands for the Holy Trinity. A straight line, ribbon or belt encircling the egg pictures God's

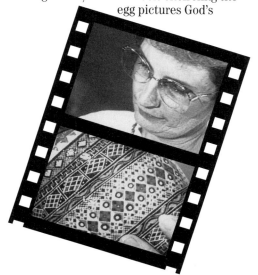

unending love, the unbroken thread of life, or family harmony or love.

There are other meanings: wolves' teeth, loyalty, wisdom and a firm grip; water, wealth; sun, the source of life. Flowers also can mean life, growth, children, charity and good will. A vine means fulfillment of wishes.

"They're kind of prayers, little individual prayers."

Colors also have special meaning. White stands for purity; yellow: moon and stars, a successful harvest and wisdom; green: spring, rebirth of nature, freshness, untouched happiness, health and innocence. There are meanings for every color in the rainbow.

Marilyn, the adopted daughter of the late Mr. and Mrs. O.B. Hartzell, Topeka business people, doesn't have a drop of Ukrainian blood, so far as she knows. She learned egg art in an unlikely place — at a gun show.

"I consider this a gift of the Lord. I've always worked with my hands, but a few years ago I developed nerve damage in my elbow. It limited my arm movements, and I couldn't do the things I used to. I went with my husband, Joe, to the gun show and I met a woman who does Ukrainian eggs. She showed me, on half of one of her little eggs, how to do it and she gave me a stylus and a block of beeswax. I went off and basically taught myself by trial and error."

She has read everything she can find on the ancient art and learns from every other source she can find.

"Very few people do this around here now, and I don't know of anyone who produces eggs in the quantity and quality that I do."

First, she applies wax on an area that she wants to protect from the dye. She might start with the basic color of the egg, or yellow, the lightest dye in her spectrum. Then she goes on from light to dark, applying wax then dunking the egg. If black is used, it is the final color. When the egg is dry, she burns off the wax with a candle, a tricky step. Finally, she applies a coat of varnish for protection and sheen.

Each winter Marilyn produces about 200 of the intricately decorated eggs and sells them for $26 or more at art and crafts shows during the spring, summer and

Cain uses stylus and wax to give life to her creations.

fall. She uses finch eggs (about the size of a jellybean) as well as those from chickens, geese, ducks, bobwhite guineas, Hungarian partridges and ostriches. The ostrich eggs are imported from Africa.

Joe, who is retired from Vulcan Chemicals, is an integral part of the operation. He makes a tiny hole in the egg and blows out the contents with air and water. The only exception is the ostrich eggs, which already have the contents removed. Joe also is manager of Marilyn's display in shows, and is producer of the two annual Harvest of the Arts festivals the couple puts on in Century II in June and October. They started the shows in 1990.

Marilyn, reared in Topeka, was a military wife who moved from base to base for 23 years until her husband brought her to Wichita on New Year's Eve 1979. He left her and their two daughters there and informed her he wanted a divorce so he could marry a younger woman. Mutual friends eventually introduced her to Joe, who was a single father. They were married Aug. 16, 1984.

"Without faith in the Lord I couldn't have made it through that terrible time after we moved to Wichita. I believe the Lord brought Joe and me together, and he has led me through my work with the eggs, and now to our Harvest of Arts festival."

Snapshot Biography

Marilyn Cain was born in Topeka on Sept. 26, 1938. She graduated from Seaman High School in Topeka, but never took art courses. She married Joe Cain Aug. 16, 1984. She has two daughters, three stepchildren, three grandsons and three step-grandsons. Years in Kansas: 32.

Garry Trudeau's Finishing Artist

Don Carlton of Kansas City says being a little crazy helps

A newspaper in front of this Kansas City home waits to be read. A cat waits to be noticed and upstairs, newspaper deadlines wait for no one.

In the studio, Don Carlton's fax machine regularly brings him the pencil drawings of Doonesbury cartoonist Garry Trudeau. Carlton, Trudeau's finishing artist, inks in the pencil lines and delivers the strips to nearby Universal Press Syndicate, which discovered Trudeau in 1970.

A year later, a Universal Press Syndicate partner suggested Carlton as a finishing artist and he has been applying ink to Zonker, Joanie and Doonesbury's large cast of characters for two decades.

"Garry's a unique individual. I think probably I am, too. In the sense of when it comes to the strip and general outlook on life, I think we share an awful lot, the same sort of bafflement about things, the inconsistencies of ourselves."

When Carlton began working for Trudeau, the fledgling strip had grown from 28 to 140 newspapers in just one year. That number has now swelled to 900 newspapers, making it one of the most popular — and most controversial — in the country.

"I liked it as a good college strip. No way did I think it would grow into this. Not because it wasn't good, but it was ground-breaking. . . . Truthfully, I didn't think newspapers would buy it."

But newspapers at the time were trying to find a comic strip that expressed the alienated youth of the late 1960s and early 1970s, and Doonesbury has filled that role for two decades, poking fun at everyone from presidents to popes.

"Garry can get away with touching topics few others can. . . . I marvel at his ability to touch on subjects that have a ring of truth to them."

Though Carlton has a degree in graphic design and experience as a newspaper artist and a technical illustrator, he's not sure what else qualifies him for the position with Trudeau except "you have to be a little crazy."

"I don't know anyone else who does what I do. Garry's arrangement with me is fairly unique."

Another requirement is to be able to handle the madness of deadlines. While most cartoonists work six weeks ahead, Trudeau has a lead time of only a week and a half so that his strips will be more timely — and he is likely to make revisions up to the deadline. Though their offices are half a continent apart, they are able to meet their deadlines by communicating via fax and phone.

In addition to outlining Trudeau's daily strips in black ink, Carlton also codes the Sunday strips in a paint-by-number system that shows the printer which colors go where.

Carlton also has completed finishing work on drawings that will be reproduced on the first line of Doonesbury products. While Trudeau long resisted the idea of Doonesbury products, he has acquiesced, with the stipulation his profits will go to charity. He also has chosen what he feels is an appropriate catalog title: "The Great Doonesbury Sell-Out." A quarter million copies were to be mailed in fall 1991.

In summer 1991, Carlton began work for another Universal Press Syndicate cartoon strip, The Far Side. His job is to apply the shading to the original drawings by cartoonist Gary Larson, creator of the slightly quirky cartoon strip.

Over the years, Carlton has come to know Trudeau and Doonesbury's large cast of characters very well. The sabbatical Trudeau took several years ago was to let "the characters develop some kind of life of their own."

"He respects the characters . . . . It sounds like a cliche, but their personalities write the strip."

Carlton has also come to know the complexity of the strips and its characters.

"I really like almost all the characters in the strip except Uncle Duke. Nobody in their right mind would like Uncle Duke. Duke's motivations are actually quite simple: greed and hedonism and the fast buck . . . . He's kind of a revelation occasionally, despite his rather lackadaisical attitude about life. His nephew is a rather moralistic sort of person from time to time. I don't get bored with the characters in this strip. They do have personalities that are very keenly and cleverly drawn that I think I understand, so they become almost friend-like themselves."

While he professes to have no favorites, he admits there are some of Doonesbury's many characters he'd like to draw more often.

"There are a few I'd kind of like to see more often. . . . There's so many characters standing in the wings waiting to get on."

There's one aspect of the strip he doesn't miss since its disappearance: the Persian Gulf War. But his reasons differ from most Americans.

"I'm sure glad we got out of Desert Storm. If I had to draw one more camouflage uniform . . . ."

"He respects the characters . . . . It sounds like a cliche, but their personalities write the strip."

Carlton applies ink to Doonesbury cast on pencil-drawn strips that are faxed to him by creator Garry Trudeau.

Snapshot Biography

Don Carlton was born Dec. 28, 1936, in Iowa Park, Texas. He graduated from Fort Worth Technical High School in 1954 and completed a bachelor's degree in graphic design at Texas Christian University in 1960. He and wife Joan have three children: Brendan, 26; Joel, 24; and Rachel, 21. Years in Kansas: 26.

Roaring into the '20s

John Cyphert of Wichita was born 50 years too late

Cyphert looks through a music book for his player piano, which he is trying to learn to play.

Although the seconds on an art deco clock continue to tick away in John Cyphert's Wichita home, some would say time was standing still rather than going forward.

"It would be nice to go back to the twenties. I would certainly be the first person in line."

Almost everything in John's house is from that period, from the player piano in the living room to the Model T in the garage and the 1920s clothes in his closet. Even the magazines, newspapers and music are from the Roaring Twenties.

"They were just an interesting period. They weren't any better than the eighties, any worse, really. They were just a comfortable period for me."

For nine years after graduating from college John worked at the Wichita Historical Museum, building exhibits and immersing himself in the city's history. And now his home is furnished with some of that history from the 1920s.

As far as modern conveniences such as electricity and gas he's glad the 1920s had them, but the furniture was not all that comfortable.

"It's mostly mission oak which is like sitting on a picket fence, it's a little too upright. It's all right for someone coming over for tea.

"If you get picky about it, the 1920s were not a lot different. There were gas stoves, electric ice boxes."

He started collecting the 1920s items during the 1970s before they were in demand and were more reasonably priced.

"Actually, my main interest was 1890 to 1930, but at that time no one else was collecting 1920s and I needed furniture. Then I met these nuts in San Francisco who lived in the 1920s, totally.

"Now the 'yuppies' are starting to get into 1920s furniture. At first nobody wanted it, now they're realizing it's nice stuff."

He bought three-fourths of the furnishings in Wichita, where art deco had just begun appearing in the 1920s. It was acquired at estate sales, auctions and from people who wanted to get rid of it.

"I don't think I paid more than $100 for anything except the piano."

He has 200 rolls for the player piano, which he is trying to learn to play. Another favorite possession is an Edison phonograph and its 500 phonograph records, especially the ragtime and early jazz ones.

"People my age can't understand why I do it."

Ninety-nine percent of the furnishings in his two-bedroom bungalow came from the 1920s. The other one percent?

"A TV and VCR," he confesses. *"I watch 1920s stuff on them."*

For a long while he didn't even own such modern conveniences, but he's made those concessions to the 1990s. And he does have another car in addition to his Model T.

"Sometimes the Model T isn't fast enough."

"They were just an interesting period. They weren't any better than the eighties, any worse, really. They were just a comfortable period for me."

Cyphert with his Model T – he does have another car.

Snapshot Biography

John Cyphert was born in Wichita on May 13, 1958. He graduated from Bishop Carroll High School in 1976 and earned a degree in graphic arts from Wichita State University in 1981. He now does restoration for the Scottish Rite Temple in Wichita. Years in Kansas: 33.

Dance Teacher Goes Underground

Ellinwood's Adrianna Dierolf found key to city's past

The Dick Building at the corner of Main Street and U.S. 56 in Ellinwood was built in 1887. Adrianna Dierolf inherited the building after the death of her last uncle. To the casual observer, there's nothing different about this 19th century building. But Adrianna knows differently.

One day in 1981 Adrianna was cleaning a basement in the building and found clues of a harness shop operation. A friend helping her clean recalled getting a haircut underground decades ago. Then a tunnel was discovered.

"People would never know, just walking down this street, that they have been walking over tunnels for years and years."

In the late 1880s, about 15 years after Ellinwood was founded in 1872, city leaders decided to expand downward. They built tunnels connecting businesses that included a barber shop, a saloon, a bathhouse, a house of ill repute, a harness shop and possibly a restaurant and grocery store.

The connecting tunnels started at the Dick Building and extended a quarter of a mile, taking several turns as the city grew. Some of the tunnels were discovered with the assistance of a water diviner.

"Now this room we feel, was the bathhouse, connected to the barber shop, as all cowboy centers were known to have in the early days. We found on this window sill, someone had

figured their wages . . Oct. 30, 1889, a dollar and a half."

Historians believe the underground was built both to save money and to provide shelter from the elements — the Kansas wind, heat and cold — that would have been very punishing to someone in an uninsulated, above-ground 19th-century building.

"They may have seen it as a way to be protected from blizzards, tornadoes and prairie fires. The heritage of many of the people was German, and Germany has always had a lot of tunnels."

The other side of one wall was found to contain a tunnel that has been traced to the old train depot, to a dance hall of that period and to a mill that operated in the late 1800s.

"You feel like you're turning back the clock of time when you're down here."

The year before the tunnel discovery, Adrianna had become involved in historical research when asked to help in a project for her church, St. Joseph's Catholic Church. She is secretary of the Ellinwood Historical Society.

A former ballet and ballroom dance teacher, Adrianna has been involved in music all her life. She met her husband, Dan, while entertaining at the Great Bend Air Base during World War II. She has sung in the church choir for 50 years, and still plays piano and organ for various church and community groups.

But for the past 10 years, Adrianna has found herself spending more and more of her time going underground.

The tunnels were first shown locally in 1982. Newspaper publicity and a feature on KAKE-TV sparked more and more visitors. Now, the total number of visitors who have met Adrianna in the alleyway to take the tour exceeds 11,000. The underground town has been the subject of national television and newspaper features, and scholars have come to view this authentic piece of prairie history.

"There were many other towns on the plains with underground buildings and tunnels. We're just fortunate to have this restored."

Today, visitors simply call up Adrianna Dierolf to

Dierolf in a tunnel under city's sidewalks.

make an appointment for a tour (316-564-2339), but soon she believes that interest by the state and city will enable her to turn over operation of the tours to the City of Ellinwood.

As you walk through the rooms with beams hexed by axe, and ceiling and floor constructed in the tongue and groove system, you can almost hear the voices of the lively characters who once spent time here.

"There's bullet holes that came from a muzzle, there was gambling here, and it was a place to go during prohibition."

The research indicates the tunnels were closed in the late 1920s, but today they're open so you can step back in time 100 years.

"Kansas has missed the boat for too many years on preserving and appreciating its history. We've found tourists from all over the world are really interested."

Dierolf leads a tour of underground tunnels that connected several Ellinwood businesses in late 1880s.

Snapshot Biography

Adrianna Dierolf was born July 7, 1918 in Ellinwood, attended schools in Ellinwood and graduated in 1936. She played piano for a dance group that summer, and ended up taking over the group when the teacher left. She studied dance under Carl Maybach of Great Bend and taught for 10 years. Her group toured cities throughout the state. She married her husband, Dan Dierolf, in 1946 and moved to San Antonio for two years before returning to Ellinwood. She has been active in Girl Scouts, Meals on Wheels and her church. Years in Kansas: 71.

Sax Player Reaches for the Stars
Bryne Donaldson of Ark City plays music that warms the heart

All of us have dreams. Some of us give up on them, while others wait but never give up. Arkansas City's Bryne Donaldson is one person who keeps his priorities on the basics of life, but never loses sight of his dream — to become a professional saxophone player.

Bryne (pronounced Bryan) had a chance to turn professional in Las Vegas in the 1980s, but he turned it down. He performed at the Maxim Hotel, and had offers to stay, but headed back to Kansas. After he returned, promoters called again. The answer was the same.

"All I could think of were my kids back home."

His children were his music. They've grown up now, and Bryne has a little more time to pursue his dream.

The dream is still tethered by reality and Bryne's full-time job as a backhoe operator and truck driver for Total Pipeline Corp. At work, the parking lot is his stage, the truck cab his concert hall.

"On lunch breaks I have an opportunity to practice."

Bryne's boss is tolerant enough to let him practice sometimes even while they're driving.

"I play as we drive down the Interstate sometimes. I can play with every song. Sometimes at work, they used to laugh when I practiced, but now they're pretty positive about it."

And when you hear Bryne Donaldson, you know his dream is reachable. The tenor sax may be cool to the touch, but the music Bryne produces warms the heart.

"It's something you can't explain. I usually play what feels good at the time. I play a lot of gospel things to myself because I'm thinking I know God is my help, and to obtain any kind of success, it will come from Him."

The Arkansas City native started playing the clarinet in grade school, then switched to the saxophone in high school. At Cowley County Community College, he earned an associate degree in music.

If Bryne gets his showbiz break someday, he would like to provide first for his mother Betty, who must be driven from Arkansas City to Wichita three times a week to undergo kidney dialysis treatments.

"She's a strong lady, she's fought for a long time. If my dream would come through with my music, I would like to see some type of private set-up for my mom and dad so my dad could enjoy his time off, to go fishing without worrying about Mother."

There is never enough time. Bryne practices every day. His fingers move gently over the sax. In the last few years, he's developed a special rendition of the "Star Spangled Banner" and taken it to rodeos and other outdoor events. Bryne also raises and trains race horses, and he's trained one horse to perform in costume with him.

Now remarried, Bryne met his wife Diane, a nurse, while being treated for an injury suffered when he was breaking horses. The Donaldsons show their appreciation to the Arkansas City community by hosting a free "Unity Concert" each year.

At the concerts, he plays to a crowded house and an appreciative audience. All those noontime practices pay off, Bryne says, with the thanks he gets each time he performs.

"I feel that it's something I excel in and if I keep working, then someday God might bless me . . . . It might happen."

Bryne is active in the Church of God in Christ, has played for out-of-state conventions and is working on a gospel album.

And even if he never gets that big break, Bryne

Bryne Donaldson plays the "Star Spangled Banner" atop horse.

Donaldson takes satisfaction that in his appearances in Kansas and nearby states, his music has made thousands of people happier.

Bryne Donaldson works as a truck driver and backhoe operator, but still manages to get in some practice time.

Snapshot Biography

Bryne Donaldson was born on July 28, 1952, in Arkansas City and graduated from high school there. He holds an associate degree in music from Cowley County Community College. He has two children, a daughter, Tracy, 18, and a stepson, Darrell, 19. Bryne and his wife, Diane, were married on Dec. 1, 1990. Years in Kansas: 39.

Teacher of Minds, Healer of Spirits
Kathleen Easter inspires sick children at Wichita's St. Francis Med Center

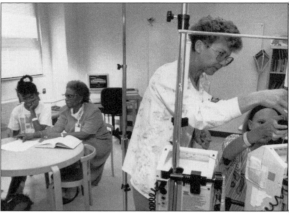

Kathleen Easter teaches children in a classroom as well as in their hospital rooms.

Hospitals can be scary places, full of good news, full of bad news. But they can also bring people together, people who need each other. For a quarter century, Kathleen Easter has been needed by hundreds of sick children in St. Francis Regional Medical Center. Some survived to come back and visit their teacher in future years, but many have died, succumbing to brutal bouts with cancer.

"I gain a lot of strength from these kids and over the years I've formed a lot of friendships with the children and their parents and it's really a joy working with them."

In the mornings, she teaches groups of about six or seven children in a classroom that houses books, other resources and two computers. In the afternoon, she gives individual attention to those who can't leave their beds. Sometimes she reads to them.

"I was reading 'The Miracle Worker' to him, and he told me that when he got to heaven he was going to tell God about me.

"There are a few tears here, especially when you get attached to the children and then you lose them; it's really heart-breaking."

Mrs. Easter gets to know not only the children, but their parents, often becoming part of their family.

"Sometimes the children don't want to confide their feelings to a doctor or nurse, but they'll talk to me."

After earning her bachelor's and master's degrees in education at Pittsburg State University, she taught in Joplin, Mo., schools before moving to Wichita with her husband in 1951. She had taught children from elementary levels to high school, which helped prepare her for her work at St. Francis, beginning in 1966.

Over the years, she developed ways that helped her to cope with the job's challenges.

"I have a strong faith and I pray a lot and I say special prayers for that child. You have to have a strong faith."

And there are ways the children have helped her.

"I was diagnosed with cancer . . . and I think the strength I've gained from all these kids helped me go through the treatment. . . . The best therapy you can have is to be around these children and to see the strength that they maintain through their illness."

The children also have given her a different perspective on her own life.

"It gives me an inner strength that I'm able to keep my life going, that no matter what, things could always be worse. . . . You can't help but know what they're going through and you think the things in your life can't compare with what the kids here suffer."

Compared to other teachers who watch their pupils grow up and go on to college and careers, Mrs. Easter has a very difficult task.

"Last September I started counting the kids lost during the year I'd been close to. I counted about seven. It makes it very difficult."

She has found that even the children with terminal diseases enjoy their schoolwork in the hospital, even the homework she assigns.

"They just get tired of all the medicine. They look forward to this. A lot keep going with their studies until the very last."

"There are a few tears here, especially when you get attached to the children and then you lose them; it's really heart-breaking."

Kathleen Easter goes over a geography lesson with Burnay "Nugget" Young, left, and Kimberly Pohlman. Nugget, 15, has been a student off and on of Mrs. Easter's for more than 10 years. "She's tough," Mrs. Easter said.

Snapshot Biography

Kathleen Easter was born April 27, 1924, in Pittsburg. She earned a B.A. from Pittsburg State University in 1946 and completed a master's in education the next year. In 1950, she married James Easter, who died in 1986. They had three children: Deborah, James and Timothy, and four grandchildren. Years in Kansas: 61.

Old Flick's World is Film and Books

Jim Erickson splices work, home and fun into one long reel

He is known to radio listeners and TV viewers as Old Flick, the movie reviewer, or as Leonard Kratzlow pushing potato chips, or as a mobile home salesman. But out on the campus of Wichita State University, he is Dr. Jim Erickson, English professor and collector of tapes, movie posters, odd signs, comic books and thousands of other books he just never gets around to reading.

"Well, some people claim that all collecting is a result of an insecure person trying to provide a secure world that he can control that's permanent, but it's just interesting stuff, like this repeating rubber gun. Not many people have ever seen one of those. And partly because every time I get rid of something, in two weeks, I have to get it back, and it always costs more."

Entering Erickson's home is like walking into the past. Even his kitchen breeds movie posters and paraphernalia that he's collected. His icebox boasts a poster of a shark that would make you think twice before opening it for a midnight snack.

There's hardly a square-inch in this man's home that isn't covered with something, what with the party decorations from his famous parties given over the past two decades.

"I realized after a while there was no use taking them down," he said, gesturing to Halloween streamers from years gone by.

It's kind of like living in the memories of some great parties, but the movie poster area is a reminder of work.

"Now this was supposed to be my total escape area where you get out of the real world into the tinsel and gossamer of Hollywood."

But after he started teaching a course on narrative in literature and film, the poster room no longer worked as an escape from work.

"It keeps reminding me of my job."

But for Erickson, it's hard to tell where work ends and fun begins. His television career was launched in the late 1960s on KAKE-TV, when then general manager Martin Umansky approached Erickson about going on television after meeting him through Community Theatre.

To thousands of Wichita area residents, he is still known as "Old Flick," the name he took for the wacky character who introduced movies on late-night TV.

Over the years, the movie posters in Erickson's house kept growing until he gave up on having a regular wall. And the books just kept coming in the door. He even built an addition to his house to hold them.

"Oh, people always ask me whether I read all these, but these are tools. When a man buys a socket set, do you ask him if he uses them all? You'd be surprised as a matter of fact how many of these have been used, but not read."

Erickson is an accomplished stage actor, and has delighted Wichita audiences for years on the stage of Commedia and Gridiron, two locally produced satirical political and social reviews.

Then there's his weekly taping of movie reviews for KMUW-FM, the university's public radio station, and for Brite Voice Systems, a telephone information system. And for public television station KPTS, Erickson hosts a Saturday night series on Hollywood classics from the 1930s and 1940s.

And if that's not enough to keep him busy, there's the weekly volleyball games he organizes, his weekly

Erickson's at home in front of a TV camera while hosting a saturday night series on Hollywood classics.

film society meetings, and, oh yes, he's still an English professor, and much of his time is spent in the crowded confines of his office grading papers.

The students have changed a lot since he first came to WSU in 1964. They're more concerned with careers and less with the world of ideas, Dr. Erickson says.

And the professor has changed, too. He doesn't host as many parties — "On Sept. 9, 1974, I quit smoking and on July 8, 1988, I quit drinking." And his collecting bent has taken more of a turn to garage sales, to the tune of $60 a week. Yet in typical Erickson fashion, his garage sale haunts have a dual purpose: He starts out intent on riding his bicycle, but then he sees a yard sign, and well . . . .

"I figure it's a harmless addiction. And sometimes there are some real finds. Some people might say it's silly to buy a book or an album or a tape you never open, but I get a certain satisfaction in ownership."

Erickson at home in his library: Lots of books have been used but not read.

Snapshot Biography

Jim Erickson was born on Dec. 14, 1931, in Minneapolis, Minn. After graduating from high school there, he served in the U.S. Marines, where his tour of duty took him to Korea for one year during the Korean War. Between 1952 and 1961, he earned a bachelors, masters and doctorate degrees in English at the University of Minnesota. He taught at the University of Texas in Austin for three years and joined the WSU faculty in 1964. Years in Kansas: 27.

The Snake Man of Lawrence

Dr. Henry Fitch courted wife 45 years and five snakebites ago

Benjamin Fitch, 5, watches his grandfather, Dr. Henry Fitch, remove a snake from a trap.

Snakes are among the most feared of creatures. Fortunately, for those of who who get the jitters when a snake starts to slither, there are some people who enjoy studying these fascinating reptiles. Henry Fitch, known as the "Snake Man of Lawrence," is one such person.

Dr. Fitch, a University of Kansas professor emeritus of ecology, is considered one of the nation's foremost authorities on reptiles. For the past 35 years, he has weighed, sexed, measured and clipped the scales of thousands of snakes in northeast Kansas. It is nothing for him to hold a deadly copperhead with one hand and write notes about it with the other.

He has been bitten four times by rattlesnakes or copperheads captured in the wild but, under the circumstances, he expected to be nipped a few times. His first "real" snakebite, in the summer of 1991, surprised him.

"I was moving boards behind the garage at home and felt a sharp sting on my left index finger. I moved a board over and there was a little copperhead beneath it. But it was a very mild bite. Apparently, only one fang penetrated."

He mentally weighed the size of the snake, estimated the poison injected and weighed those results against the reaction he knew would come from the antivenin. He decided against treatment.

"After a few minutes, I was reassured about that (decision) because I did not get violently sick to the stomach as I had the other times . . . . I guess the lesson is I should have been thinking about snakes and you should never, never reach where you can't see."

Dr. Fitch has been watching where he reached for most of his adult life. Even as a rodent ecologist for the U.S. Bureau of Biological Survey in Yosemite National Park and in Louisiana, he was always reaching for snakes. He continued that hobby when he became the first ecology instructor at the University of Kansas.

"I wasn't invited to KU to be a snake man, though. The position was to be in charge of the reservation area, which is maintained as a natural area just like a national park — free from human disturbance — and also to teach at the university."

In his spare time, he tramped through pastures and woods, trapping and examining all sorts of snakes, from benign blue racers to bad-tempered timber rattlers. Snakes became both his vocation and his avocation, and he passed that fascination on to his family.

He taught his wife, Virginia, their children and five grandchildren the fine art of snake-catching. Two of the children, John and Alice, became field biologists. And he still shares his knowledge enthusiastically with the students.

"Over the years, I've had a great many school groups here and one of my goals is to try to put to rest any fear they may have of snakes and get them to handle harmless little snakes. It's partly the reaction of their elders, but also I think there is a tendency for people to have a natural fear. I consider myself lucky to have been born without it."

Fitch also considers himself lucky to have spent a lifetime doing what he loves most. When he's not peering down a snake's throat, he lives quietly with his wife on the natural-history reservation, where he has stayed on as curator. In their home, they keep the copperhead that has been with them for the past 10 years. It, of course, it is in a cage.

"It's not tame at all. It's just as dangerous as freshly caught because it's a big one and doesn't like being handled."

He had hoped to breed it with a "remarkable" mutant copperhead that had none of the band markings typical of the breed. The mutant died without bearing any patternless young, and Fitch still hopes to find another mutant to study.

Whether he does or not will have no effect on the pleasure that stalking snakes has always brought him.

"I never regretted it. I wouldn't change a thing. In general, I think that people who work with animals in the field, whether snakes or birds or rodents or monkeys, find it deeply satisfying and wouldn't trade it for any other kind of career — even though it may not be very rewarding financially."

SNAPSHOT BIOGRAPHY

Henry Fitch was born in Medford, Ore. on Dec. 25, 1909. He earned a B.A. degree from the University of Oregon in 1930 and a few years later completed both M.A. and Ph.D. degrees at the University of California-Berkeley. He was married Sept. 6, 1946, to a woman he had taken snake hunting during their courtship. He and Virginia have three children, John and Chester Fitch and Alice Echelle, and five grandchildren. Years in Kansas: 43.

Fitch and one of his snakes. He and wife Virginia even went snake hunting while courting.

Hometown Girl Makes It to the Big Show

Wichita's Dana Fleming balances home life with demands of network TV

"They loved it when I talked about Kansas." Dana at Home.

Dana Fleming of Wichita always knew she wasn't cut out for a nine-to-five job, so she looked at her options and decided she would go into television, radio or magazine writing.

It turned out to be television. She studied, she worked at local stations, and in 1981 she began climbing the stairs that took her, from 1990-91, to ABC's national morning TV program, "The Home Show." It was not an eight-hour job. It was more like 15 hours a day, and she and her family lived a hectic life, commuting between Los Angeles and Wichita, for 18 months until network politics took her off the show July 5, 1991. But her climb in national TV has not ended.

"I'm in the middle of a big hunt," she said shortly after moving back to Wichita. "Lots of people have ideas for shows that would revolve around me, and I'm flying to Los Angeles or New York every week or every third week to talk with the head Poohbahs of networks, syndicators."

If the right project comes along, it will have to include more time in Wichita, and time for her family: husband Larry, daughter Rebecca, 5, and son David, 2. During her time on "The Home Show," she and the children lived in a rented Los Angeles house. Larry, a Wichita entrepreneur, would join them several days a week, and Dana and the children would fly to Wichita to spend one weekend a month – a tiring routine.

But things hadn't slowed down noticeably several weeks after her return to Wichita. Even when she was growing up in Wichita as Dana Hilger, she was unafraid of demanding schedules.

"When I was at WSU I worked 40 hours a week as promotion assistant at Channel 12 while I was taking 15 hours of classes. That was in 1978."

As a student at Kapaun Mount Carmel High School, she was busy with activities and was homecoming queen one year. At WSU, she was a cheerleader in addition to all her other activities. In keeping with her ambition, she added minors in broadcast journalism and speech communication to her major, English literature.

After graduating in 1979, she became a promotion assistant at KAKE-TV, where she made some "embarrassing" commercials in addition to other duties.

"I never wanted to be on camera. Only because of prodding from Martin Umansky (then general manager of the station) did I ever end up on camera."

Her first assignment was to do a Kansas segment on KAKE-TV's "PM Magazine." Then she was tapped to be co-host of Kansas City's "PM Magazine" (1981-1983) and from there moved to Philadelphia, the fourth-largest TV market in the country, to host a live talk show from 1983 to 1985. Then HBO hired her to do entertainment news. She was in that post when ABC asked her to co-host "The Home Show."

"I learned from each of the shows. At 'PM' I learned how to produce stories and to memorize. In Philadelphia I learned how to do live television."

At "The Home Show" she found a program that suited her down-home personality and her dedication to home and family. The producer was willing to listen to ideas she had for Kansas-based stories. The show

went to Hesston on the first anniversary of the 1990 tornado and had stories about the 1991 Andover tornado and the Wichita River Festival. Dana did live coverage from Wichita on the 1991 Miss USA Pageant.

"For the Andover tornado, we talked with my mother, Lee Thompson, who lived there. Fortunately her house was not hit. Oh, and let me tell you about Mother's Day in 1990. We had Larry Hatteberg (KAKE anchor) pick up flowers and take them to her at her job, while a live camera showed the whole thing on national TV. They loved it when I talked about Kansas."

After she started on "The Home Show," Dana found herself recognized wherever she went.

"It shocked me. I would think, they know me. Did I go to school with them? The beauty of 'The Home Show' was that people identified with me. They would say, 'You're just like I am. You have problems just like I do.'"

Despite all the attention, Dana has retained the hometown girl personality. For her, being on national television is a humbling experience.

"Every nuance of your face, the way you speak, or talk with your hands too much . . . you see. It's embarrassing and you never get over it."

She and Larry Fleming met in 1980, when she was doing promotion for his Wendy's restaurant. They married in 1984. Rebecca came along in 1985 and David in 1989. Dana is working hard on her career, but she makes no secret of the fact that her family comes first.

"I'm a wife and a mom number one, and if the television thing can fit in there, great. I would love to have another child. Larry thinks it's perfect the way it is. We'll see. We're in negotiations. My whole life is a series of negotiations."

"They loved it when I talked about Kansas."

Dana Fleming descends the stairs with her children Rebecca and David.

Snapshot Biography

Dana Fleming was born March 8, 1955, in Wichita. She attended Kapaun Mount Carmel and Wichita State University. She married Larry Fleming Aug. 25, 1984, and they have two children. Years in Kansas: 27.

Bringing a Log Cabin Back to Life
Augusta's Doylene Foreman works to see we never forget our heritage

Wood and mortar show time's decay. It's an old building: 1868 to be exact. History lives in the generations of settlers who used this building — the preachers, schoolchildren and shopkeepers, the hardy pioneers who helped build Augusta. And people like Doylene Foreman want to make sure we never forget our heritage.

"That's the thing I think about the most . . . what type of people were they?"

Doylene is the director of the Augusta Historical Society and oversees the ongoing restoration of the log building – one of only two in Kansas still in its original location. The other is in Junction City.

"I've been very fascinated with the cellar and the way they just laid the logs down on the ground and built from the ground up. Not the way we do it today.

"Many of my ancestors were early settlers here in Kansas and they lived in log houses. My grandparents lived in log houses. So, I often think about what life must have been like for them in that time.

"The Indians left and this became a trading post and a general store. It was also used by the Methodists, the Baptists and the Masons."

Doylene has been instrumental in restoring Augusta's Historical Museum as a living monument to the past.

"We have a lot more people who have become interested in the museum and in the log house since we began our restoration."

In 1941, the historical society bought the building, took the siding off and began the restoration work. In 1986, 118 years after C.N. James erected the building made of hewn cottonwood logs, 12- to 14-inches thick, Doylene got involved in the museum. It was a time when the museum boosters were considering expanding the office hours, promotional efforts and restoration work.

"I started doing this just for fun. Then I convinced them they should let me straighten it out. It wasn't open very many hours."

But history isn't confined to Doylene's work. Her own home was built in 1886.

"The house we bought, there are so many beautiful things in it when you start to strip away the paint that's been put on it for years. And they have a lot of character to them that the new homes don't have.

"I did research to see who owned it, then more research on the lives of those people, interviewing people who knew them and going through newspaper clips. So I wrote a book that goes with the house."

But it is at the museum at 303 State St. (316-775-5655), among the display cases of Augusta's history, that Doylene feels her community spirit.

"Well, this old boot and shoe were found when they were digging up the foundation of the log house. They found this underneath. It's very exciting. It's very special."

And history is special. More and more, she and the Augusta Historical Museum Board are convincing townspeople to support the museum and log building project, and visitors come from many states across the nation.

Doylene Foreman holds the boots dug up from the foundation of the log house.

"I believe that we cannot better ourselves for tomorrow, unless we know about our yesterdays."

Doylene Forman takes a big step back in time in this photograph taken in one of the living areas of the two-story structure constructed in 1868.

Snapshot Biography

Doylene Foreman was born Dec. 25, 1946, in Norton, where she graduated from high school in 1964. She attended business college in Salina and Butler County Community College. She moved to Wichita in 1966. On Dec. 13, 1976, Doylene and her family survived a tornado that hit their house. She has two daughters by her first marriage: Kimberly, 21, and Tamara, 18. She moved to Augusta in 1985 and married Eldon Foreman in 1986. Years in Kansas: 44.

In Gandhi's Shadow

Dr. Shanti Gandhi of Topeka respects his family heritage

Most of the world will know the great Gandhi and his non-violent teachings only through history books or movies. But one of the most memorable experiences of a Topeka heart surgeon is spending three months, at the age of 7, traveling around southern India with Gandhi — his great-grandfather, who was tragically assassinated only a year later.

Gandhi's India is half a world and nearly half a century away from Topeka, but Dr. Shanti Gandhi hopes someday to take his four daughters back to his native country to learn more about their ancestor.

"We read and heard about him. I knew he was important, but I didn't know why."

As he grew up, he understood the relevance of Gandhi's teachings, which he considers just as valid today.

"His philosophy was unique, age old, from the time of Christ and, I think, when everybody's making nuclear weapons to wipe each other out, I think we need his philosophy today, more than any time."

Dr. Gandhi says that though he was only 8, he'll never forget Jan. 30, 1948 — the day Gandhi was assassinated in New Delhi.

"It was announced on the radio about 6 in the evening. That's one day I don't think anyone will forget."

As a boy growing up in Bombay, Shanti had no ambition to be a heart surgeon or to leave his native country.

"I have no background of noble intentions," he says, chuckling. *"It was a last-minute decision."*

His father, who often spoke of his grandfather Gandhi, was a doctor and it was not a vocation Shanti had considered — until it was time to choose a major in college.

"He talked to me only once and for a short period of time and expressed his wish that I be a doctor."

He reasoned that if his father had demanded he follow in his footsteps, he could have refused. But this way he was obligated to take the wish seriously — and it was a decision he has never regretted.

He assumed he would stay in India to practice, but the decision to become a heart surgeon changed that.

"It was very difficult in India to be a heart specialist. They were not as advanced as we are here. There was not the opportunity to do what I do here. I love what I do here."

He left for the United States after completing his M.D. degree at Grant Medical College in Bombay in 1967. After post-graduate training in Youngstown, Ohio, he was a surgeon at three Michigan hospitals and had a private practice in Ohio before moving to Topeka, where he founded the Kansas Heart Institute in 1978.

His daughters have expressed an interest in learning more about their great-great-grandfather, but Dr. Gandhi concedes that for now they're more interested in boys. While growing up, Dr. Gandhi avoided mentioning his great-grandfather because he wanted to succeed on his own merits. His daughters are now learning to field those fairly frequent inquiries as to whether they're related to *that* Gandhi.

"When you say 'yes,' they don't believe you. And if they do believe you, they don't know what to say."

Seeing the movie "Gandhi," which won Oscars for best picture, best director and best actor in 1982, helped illuminate some of the history of his great-grandfather, Dr. Gandhi says.

"I'll always be secretly proud of it. When I saw the movie, it made me realize what I was really proud of."

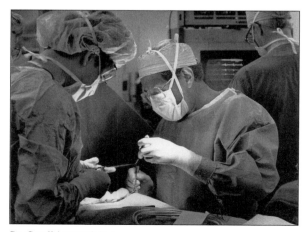

Dr. Gandhi at work in surgery.

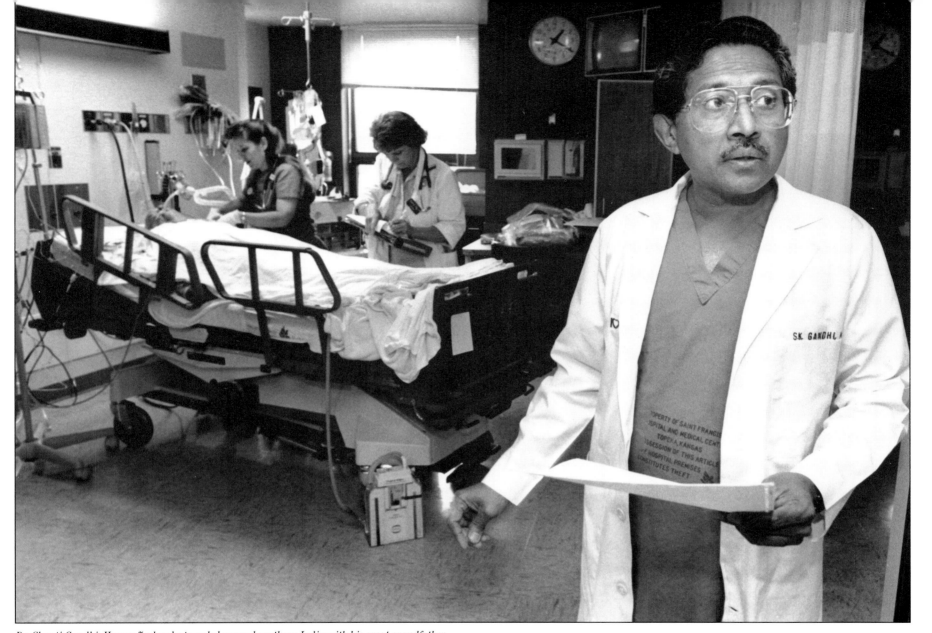

Dr. Shanti Gandhi: He was 7 when he traveled around southern India with his great-grandfather.

Snapshot Biography

Shanti Gandhi was born Feb. 10, 1940, in Kerala, India, and christened Shantikumar Kantilal Gandhi. He earned his B.S. and M.D. degrees from Grant Medical College in Bombay and then moved to Youngstown, Ohio, to study heart surgery. There, he met his future wife, Susan Jane. He was a surgeon and had a private practice before moving to Topeka to found the Kansas Heart Institute. He and his wife have four daughters: Anjali, 12; Anita, 20; Alka, 18; and Ann, 11. Years in Kansas: 13.

Keeping the Family Homestead Alive
Burden's David Gatton likes life with a wood stove and corn shucker

Nearly eight decades after being born on his grandfather's homestead, David Gatton has filled — some would say consumed — the Cowley County ranch with antiques of the past to preserve it for future generations. The hundreds of artifacts he's accumulated keep the past alive and give the ranch the aura of bygone days in Kansas.

David Gatton enjoys the privacy of rural life, a good sale and antiques. He's lived his whole life on the same land homesteaded by his grandfather from Ohio in 1873.

A sign with the painted letters "Century Farm: Owned by the same family for over 100 years" greets visitors to one of the oldest farms in the county.

As soon as visitors turn off the road, they are greeted with the dozens of antiques that line the property and the hundreds more that fill the house and the outbuildings.

When his grandfather homesteaded the land, there were 160 acres; now there's 240, and at the age of 79, Gatton still tends to it himself.

"I do it all myself. You can't hire anybody any more."

But the privacy of the rural Burden ranch certainly has many advantages.

"I'm my own boss and I do what I please."

He's darn proud of the ranch that was passed from his grandfather to his father, and then to him.

"As long as I'm able to go I'll be out here. You're not going to catch me around up there playing dominoes in town. You'll find me out here somewhere."

The 118-year-old homestead is not only stocked with cattle, chickens and cats, but hundreds of antiques that tell the story of the past century.

In the cold winter months, he likes to build a fire in an old wood stove and show visitors his old wind-up record player, the grindstones, a corn shucker, the horse-drawn farm equipment and the early-model telephone.

He got started collecting antiques after he saw some of his father's belongings sold for "a heckuva price." He's reclaimed many of his father's tools and belongings and has re-created his shop, complete with blacksmith tools and forge.

His buying binges have slowed, mostly because he's run out of room and "because there's hardly anything I don't have." But rarely does he agree to sell any of his treasures.

"I don't sell unless I have a duplicate."

He collects pieces of farm equipment from another century, many unrecognizable to city folks of today. He tinkers with them and often gets them back into running condition.

"It's a challenge, a challenge to see if I can put something together."

"I'm my own boss and I do what I please."

Snapshot Biography

David Gatton was born on his grandfather's homestead — where he still lives — on June 24, 1912. He graduated from Burden High School and "bached it a few years" before marrying his first wife, Marjorie. Following her death, he and Eva were married in 1976. He has two sons, Richard and Ronnie, and five grandchildren. Years in Kansas: 79.

Crawly Creatures Fill Her Living Room
To Marian Gault of Mission Hills, raising caterpillars preserves beauty

Caterpillars. Now most folks don't think of them as household pets. But to Marian Gault, they are all that and more. In fact, they even live in her house.

"Sometimes I think they're something only a mother could love, because, you know, they're great big worms to a lot of people. When you look at them with a unprejudiced eye, they're like jewels almost."

Taught by her mother to be a naturalist, Marian's living room is alive with these crawly creatures.

"When you're a caterpillar and you're that size, you don't move fast. It's almost slow motion. Once in a while, I'll come up with two or three butterflies flying through the living room. And that's not all bad either.

"And the first question is 'why?' Because usually people . . . when you're talking about caterpillars say, 'What does a baby butterfly look like?' And you say, 'Well it's a caterpillar is what it really is'. . . and this is where disbelief really sets in."

Marian raises monarchs, swallowtails, lunas, cecropias and pollyphemus moths.

"The pollyphemus have a peacock eye on the lower wing. They're very beautiful and special."

There was a time in her life – 27 years in fact – when Marian was without butterflies.

"Then in the late 1960s, I was at a traffic light and saw a bare tree with eight cocoons. I took them home and six hatched. Now that people know I raise them, if they find them in their garden, if there is a flicker of doubt if it's a worm or a pest, they call me. When I get a phone call, I get in the car and shoot right over there."

She also finds the eggs out in the countryside, driving along the roads, then stopping to look on the underside of leaves.

Come spring, after the caterpillars have wintered in their cocoons and undergone a metamorphosis, they become winged beauties, with a three- to five-inch wing spread. And it's the metamorphosis that Marian finds almost a miracle.

"You can't raise butterflies and have any doubt in your mind about God."

Nor, she says, can you be cynical about butterflies.

"I can't. Neither could you! No, nobody could," she said as she pointed to some with "red heads. The body is green but the head is reddish colored. They're all endangered. They're on the rare list."

Outside, nature prepares for winter. Inside Marian's house, spring is just a cocoon away.

"He's minding his own business and he doesn't know what he's going to be. He doesn't know that he's going to be anything at all. He's in for a lovely surprise."

One of Marian's biggest surprises was on a trip to Atlanta several decades ago.

"I saw a migration where thousands of butterflies went through the open windows of an office building and came out on the other side. It was something."

She also delights in releasing her harvest.

"When you turn the moths loose in the meadows, it's a wonderful experience as they begin to fly high in a lazy spiral."

Her entire backyard in Mission Hills is turned over to nature. There's milkweed, dill, fennel and Queen Ann's – good butterfly food. Pesticides are taboo.

"And we get a lot of animals our way . . . orphaned raccoons, possums, squirrels and red fox. My philosphy is: don't disturb our world.

"There's a cardinal, a baby. Yeah, I like nature. I like nature very much. They're friends, you know. They come to dinner every day, breakfast, lunch . . . bring their children."

"You can't raise butterflies and have any doubt in your mind about God."

Marian Gault with chrysalises.

Snapshot Biography

Marian Gault was born in Kansas City, Kan., on July 18, 1924. Her family moved to Michigan when she was a child, then returned to Kansas City, where she graduated from Southwest High School in Kansas City, Mo. She attended a girls' school in Mississippi, then graduated from the University of Arizona in Tucson. She spent three years in New York studying interior design, then returned to Kansas City. Years in Kansas: About 50.

From the Highest Point in Kansas

Ed and Cindy Harold watch over Mt. Sunflower near Colorado border

It's a great place to be — these wide open and some would say barren plains of western Kansas. You get a different perspective up here, looking out for miles to the distant horizon, when you're atop the highest point in Kansas, Mt. Sunflower, 4,039 feet above sea level.

Ed Harold's grandfather was born in Missouri, then followed the westward migration in 1906 to Wallace County, where he homesteaded the land where Ed and wife Cindy now live.

"It's very nice to go out on the high plains and you can see for miles," says Ed. "In Wichita or any other large city, it's difficult for you to see beyond a block or two."

A lot has changed since the land was broken nearly nine decades ago and the first wheat crop was planted.

"We raise cattle now and have land in the reserve program for grass. The land is highly erodable."

To Cindy and Ed Harold, there's beauty in the landscape — a panorama that some city folks might find a bit boring.

"You think of Kansas as brown and flat, and nothing around it," Cindy said. "You come out to this area, and it's beautiful."

A cattle gate lets cars drive up to the bottom of Mt. Sunflower. People come here from all 50 states. They even like to have breakfast up here, Ed says.

"This is a place that has some significance to Kansas and especially to the high plains. It's an area of high elevation. It means a great deal to
us every time we come up. The kids are always wanting to come up here."*

The land where Mt. Sunflower is located is next to the land Ed's grandfather homesteaded. It was purchased just after World War II.

"It gave him a high point so that he could observe all the cattle and where they were going. We're very proud of it. It's just a quirk that our family owns it and we're very glad that we do."

More than 600 visitors a year make this not-so-arduous climb up the slope. To folks from the Rockies this may not seem quite like a mountain.

"Not by definition," Cindy admits. "It doesn't have enough slope to be a real mountain. It was named Mt. Sunflower by a neighbor lady because Kansas has to have a high point for us. It's called the mount. You can just see forever."

When you do make it up to the top, there's even a place to sign in that was put up during the centennial of the nearby town of Weskan. A retired geologist discovered the spot in 1961, and a galvanized pipe was driven in the ground. Then a fence was put up and Ed hauled a rock up from the creek. There are even Wallace County Pride signs telling I-70 travelers how to get there.

"There's a little poem about the Sunflower State. It says, 'Congratulations . . . you've conquered Mt. Sunflower; from either the east or the south face, you're now standing higher than anyone in the state of Kansas.' "

And people come from all over. The registration book includes notes from Kansas City, New Orleans, Germany. Some of the notes say: "very educational, loved it, fantastic. No nosebleed."

Ed Harold looks at a register of people who have visited the mountain.

Do Ed and Cindy and the kids feel left out – way out here?

"We are by no means backwoods. My wife and I are both teachers. We're constantly on the go with school, church and cultural activities. Our friends in the city can't believe how hectic a life we lead. But I think Tatum (his daughter) would like to live in town.

"This is my heritage. This is what was passed down to me. I have a respect and love for the land. Yes, it's cold and windy in the winters and hot in the summers, but I just look at it as another day in the life of . . . the trials and tribulations of Kansas weather.

"The reward is watching things grow and green up and then the harvest. There appears to be nothing out here, but what is here is close to my heart."

And Ed keeps a sense of humor close at hand, especially when he reads the notes that are left behind.

"We get these all the time . . . . About how proud people are that they could climb the mountain without their ice axes."

The Harold family – Ed, Cindy, Tatum and Nathan – standing atop Mt. Sunflower.

Snapshot Biography

Ed Harold was born in Goodland on June 14, 1947, and raised in Weskan. He attended Colby Community College and graduated from Fort Hays State College. His wife, Cindy, was born in Kit Carson, Colo., on Oct. 25, 1951. She graduated from the University of Northern Colorado in Greeley. Ed and Cindy were married in June 1972. They have two children: a daughter, Tatum, 13, and a son, Nathan, 11. Years in Kansas: Ed, 44; Cindy, 19.

Wheat Field Muralist

Stan Herd of Lawrence gains national attention with his 160-acre portraits

For most of us, a plowed field is just that: a lot of dirt, and not much else. But if you're an artist, and your name is Stan Herd, then wheat fields and pastures could soon become a work of art.

"I think most farm boys, when they're out plowing fields, have an idea about spelling their name into the ground or something, so the idea of the big portrait came into being."

Stan's large murals already had drawn national attention by late 1981, when he traded his paint brush for a plow and carved a portrait of the Indian chief Satanta into a 160-acre Kansas field near Dodge City.

Soon after he finished, he described his technique as he showed a graph on which he had plotted the portrait.

"This is the first sketch, what we first started out with. . . . We went out and we shot centerpoint. Each one of these squares represents 200 feet. That eyeball out there would be the size of an average house, I guess. It's just a dream I've had for a long time and it finally came true."

His dream was only visible from several thousand feet in the air; he used airplanes or helicopters to monitor his progress from start to finish.

Like an engineer surveying a new road, Stan used small flags as guides for the disc he pulled behind the tractor. He referred to scale drawings he had made, but the result was visible only in Stan's mind. Before

Stan is privileged as few artists are – he literally works within his canvas.

he finished, he described the pressure he felt.

"I know this thing is feasible. I've just got to work. I've got to get it done. . . . There's been two or three times in the last two weeks out in the sun and the heat and the wind, I was just about to call her off. Seeing it this evening . . . I think it's been worth it. It gives me quite a feeling. It really does."

Next, he disced and plowed a portrait of Will Rogers into a neighboring field. He planted the portrait with milo, corn, wheat and soybeans so, as the seasons changed, the picture also became an ever-changing kaleidoscope of color. He celebrated Kansas' 125th anniversary with a bouquet of sunflowers spread over a field 600 feet wide by 1,050 feet long.

"I'm trying to utilize nature's palette. . . . You know, it's a limited palette. There's only so much I can do and only so many colors I can pull out of the land, but I keep seeing this image that I know could be. . . . As a young man watching the flight of geese in the fall, I always imagined what they might see in that pattern as they looked down in the middle of the field."

Stan has always stood out from the crowd like his field art stands out from the Kansas fields and prairies.

"I was, I don't know, proud to be different. I never wanted to blend in with the crowd, and that's an oddity in small-town America, where conformity's very important. I didn't have that sense when I was really young, but when I got my wings at 18, I loved the idea that I was not the average cat."

Stan grew up on a farm near Protection, a small town south of Dodge City. His parents strained their budget to finance art-school instruction, and their reward has been their son's success as both a muralist and a field artist.

Through television, newspapers and magazines, the world has watched Stan plow and disc and plant portraits, scenes and a bottle of Absolut vodka. As he neared 40, he said, he lost a little of his idealism and took on that commercial project as a financial cushion for his field art.

"It's kind of ironic for me that I did my artwork for 10 years and really got a lot of publicity, but the commercial project selling

vodka is the one that probably will stick in everybody's mind. . . . The only frustration I have with that is that we're in a pop culture that worships icons like Michael Jackson and Arnold Schwarzenegger and I hope that my work is never put into that. I don't try to appeal to the masses. Maybe I'm a little naive about that."

It's important to Stan to experiment with new techniques. In 1991, he tackled the Kansas prairie at Salina to create a portrait of Carol Cadue, a Kickapoo Indian princess whose father, the chief, had become embroiled in a legal battle with Kansas Attorney General Bob Stephan.

"You have to challenge yourself in life or it gets boring."

This challenge included burning a portion of the prairie, then hoping the regrowth of late summer would restore four acres burned when the fire got out of control. But these difficulties Stan takes in stride as he pursues a life-long dream.

"To me, of all the things that I could see out there as a young person, the most exciting and the most potentially rewarding, almost spiritual profession – if you want to call it that – is to be an artist. It's kind of being a preacher and a teacher and a mystic and an adventurer and an experimenter. . . and it's a mandate to remain open-minded your whole life, which is extremely hard to do when you get middle-aged. Most people's minds go shut at about 25, I think."

Stan Herd with a detailed drawing – the first step in turning pastures into a work of art.

Snapshot Biography

Stan Herd was born in Protection on July 19, 1950. He graduated from Protection High School and attended one year at Wichita State University on an art scholarship. He teaches and still takes classes occasionally at the University of Kansas in Lawrence, where he lives. He married Janis F. Light-Herd in 1984; they have one child, Evan, born in 1991. Years in Kansas: 39.

El Perico's One-Man Staff

Al Hernandez turns retirement into opportunity

Retirement turned out to be a golden opportunity not only for Wichitan Al Hernandez, but for thousands of Kansans of Hispanic heritage. The bilingual El Perico newspaper he helped found in 1977 grew to be so important to its subscribers that in early 1991, when it was in danger of folding, they came to its rescue with donations and renewed subscriptions.

"We were about to give up the first of the year. They responded pretty well."

The roles of editor, ad salesman and typesetter for the Spanish newspaper were not ones he necessarily wanted at first. But his wife was tired of having her newly retired husband underfoot all day, and of the group contemplating starting a bilingual newspaper, he was the only retired one — and besides he could type.

"They talked me into it. Seven or eight of us started it; I was the only one who was retired. They dumped it on me. I had no experience."

But he learned fast and the first four-page issue was distributed in April 1977 with support from the United Methodist Urban Ministry, which is still the publisher. For more than a decade, Al typed each Spanish and English article as it appeared in the monthly 12-page newspaper. In 1989, the paper acquired its first computer and though Al found it hard to adjust to at first, it did cut down the production time.

"About two years ago we got a computer. It made it a lot easier but it gave me a headache at first."

Al, who was born in Mexico, had learned to type while a high school student in Oklahoma, where his dad worked for the railroad. He moved to Wichita in 1938 and worked for the Cudahy meat-packing plant for 38 years until it was closed. He decided to retire, but his wife had other ideas. The first year of retirement was a difficult one, as Mary recalls:

"When he retired and stayed home that whole year, I told him, 'Either you get out and do volunteer work or I will go out and do it and you can stay home and take care of the house.'"

Al's decision was a fortunate one for the 3,500 subscribers who look forward to receiving the monthly newspaper.

"People who have moved away from Wichita have asked to have the paper mailed to them. It's going to 17 different states now."

He often hears from readers, including teachers who use the newspaper in their classrooms, and he has gained a lot of satisfaction from filling a void in the Hispanic community.

"It's so nice when you hear somebody say, 'I'm so glad you're here. It's helped us out.' That's a big encouragement."

He depends on volunteers to help translate, but other than that he fills all roles at the newspaper, from writing to paste-up. His "volunteer" job keeps him busy from about 9 a.m. to 2 or 3 p.m. every day.

Some articles and ads are called in, and some articles are taken from the Hispanic Link News Service. He doesn't pound the streets in search of advertisers, but he's always promoting El Perico.

"I try to sell where I trade. They're pretty good about it."

And, on occasion, the 78-year-old editor does think about retiring — again.

"I'm gonna stay at it 'til I can't anymore. I think I'm doing something to help the community."

"They talked me into it. Seven or eight of us started it; I was the only one who was retired. They dumped it on me. I had no experience."

Snapshot Biography

Alfonso Hernandez was born Aug. 2, 1913, in Mexico. He graduated from Blackwell (Okla.) High School in 1934 and moved to Kansas in 1938. He and his wife, Mary, who were married in 1955, have one daughter, Sylvia, and three grandchildren. Years in Kansas: 53.

Al Hernandez, busy doing what he loves.

Drugstore of Days Gone By

Hazel Holmes' smile and marble soda fountain cure Hamilton's ills

The Holmes Drugstore in Hamilton. You may never have been there, but somewhere in your past, you've been in a place just like it.

Hazel Holmes bought the place in 1951. She and her husband, Alton, had been farmers since they married in 1925. When he died 25 years later, she tried keeping up the farm for a year, with the help of a neighbor. She raised chickens and took care of the cattle and continued to do field chores as she always had. Her daughter, Donita Holmes Edwards, suggested she move to town and buy the drugstore.

"I borrowed $5,000 and paid $125 a month for three years. That's when drinks were a nickel."

Hazel is a determined lady, Donita says.

The drugstore carried the usual items, plus gifts and veterinary supplies. The old marble-based soda fountain is now covered with a red-flecked linoleum counter.

"Times were different then. This was a place where people came after the games — Saturday night, you know."

It's always Saturday night when you're young. And when you're young, the lure of penny candy is irresistible. Children have always been standard after-school customers at Holmes Drugstore. Before schools were unified, Hazel carried textbooks and school supplies for every school in Greenwood County.

"Since 1952, I've graduated a lot of kids."

Some of those kids have returned to the drug store almost daily for decades. The store opens at 6 a.m. for breakfast, caters to coffee-break crowds, serves lunch and dinner and closes at 8 p.m. — seven days a week.

Hazel, who celebrated her 92nd birthday on Sept. 16, 1991, comes in every morning around 7:30 to have breakfast. She does the bookkeeping and chats with countless friends while Donita runs the counter. Hazel is a woman who laughs easily and often.

She moves slower now, especially when her rheumatism acts up, but she still manages to flow with the times. When the Hamilton grocery store closed, she added some groceries to her stock. Brooms, lightbulbs and cleaning products also are on hand at the drugstore.

"We accommodate everybody. Everybody."

They do it, in part, because Hazel and her daughter are astute businesswomen. They know how to keep their store running while businesses in other small towns are closing.

But they also do it because their customers are their friends. For Hazel, losing the daily contact with them would be almost like losing part of her family.

"I see people every day that I wouldn't see otherwise. I know everybody, you know. No, I wouldn't retire. What would I do? I've seen these old ladies sitting in the window. You know, nothing to do but just sit there. I couldn't do that . . . . I'll just be here 'til I'm done."

Hazel philosophizing . . . one of her favorite pastimes.

"We accommodate everybody. Everybody."

Mike Schlotterbeck buys some penny candy at Hazel's store.

Myron and Iliff Nicholas visit with Hazel Holmes at her store in Hamilton.

Snapshot Biography

Hazel Holmes was born Sept. 16, 1899, at Emporia. She graduated from the eighth grade at Americus and from C.D. Long School of Business in Emporia. She married Alton Holmes on Sept. 16, 1925. Hazel has two daughters, Donita Edwards and Marjorie Ball, seven grandchildren and 11 great-grandchildren. Years in Kansas: 92.

At 84, China Painter Hasn't Slowed Down

Olya Hull of McPherson preserves the timeless art by making heirlooms

Olya Hull, an artist who makes the difficult task of china painting look easy, believes that if advancing age means going downhill, she's only picking up speed. Her McPherson home is filled with Limoges boxes, china plates, Ming urns and Victorian lamps she has painstakingly painted with finely detailed flowers, cherubs, angels, delicate portraits or scenes from centuries past.

For Olya, art does imitate her life. She has captured grandchildren and favorite scenes in the timeless art of china painting, a talent she says she was born with.

"It is a given talent. That's what they tell me, I inherited it."

She started oil painting on canvas as a teenager but later switched to painting on porcelain.

"It's dainty. I like dainty things. . . . China painting, you can put it on anything. You can have a picture, you can have a set of dishes, you can have jewelry. There's no limit to what you can do with china painting."

Both the painting and the teaching have proved therapeutic for Olya, who moved with her husband to McPherson in 1941. After he died of a heart attack in 1957, she attended business college and got a job at Farmers Alliance Insurance, where she worked until she retired. She started painting on porcelain in 1961 and started teaching others in 1973.

"I think it's nice that I teach, because if I was painting, I probably wouldn't want anybody to come. I'd want to be by myself and paint. This way I meet people and make friends."

Eighty-four-year-old Olya still teaches seven china painting classes every week. She has five students in each of the seven classes that meet in her home studio, which houses two kilns. To make sure she gives each student the same amount of individual attention, she uses a timer. It's this individual attention that has attracted students from as far away as Lyons, Salina, Council Grove and Newton for her weekly classes. Some pupils have been attending her classes for more than a decade.

"I tell my students if they're doing good work, they're making heirlooms."

Known as the "lamp lady," Olya is one of only a few who repair and repaint Victorian globe lamps, restoring the antique lamps to their original beauty.

Growing up with a wealthy stepfather and his family in Texas caused her to rebel at the age of 15. After overhearing her step-grandmother say she didn't want her to live with them, she ran away and lived with various relatives in Kansas.

"Well, they tell me I'm a rebel. I probably am a non-conformist. I like to be myself."

And she has no plans to slow down or to retire. She visits her daughter and granddaughters throughout the year and hopes to travel to Japan and visit art galleries there.

"I think a lot of people have the attitude that when they retire at 65, they're just supposed to sit in their rocking chair and be happy. I couldn't do that because I have a nervous energy, I think. I'm going to try as long as I can to stay young."

She also can't slow down because her students depend on her and because there are many paintings left to be painted.

"I have too many ideas. If I get everything done I want to, I'll be a thousand years old."

Nothing high-tech here, just talent, steady hands and a fine eye for details.

"Well, they tell me I'm a rebel. I probably am a non-conformist. I like to be myself."

"I'm just a recycled flapper."

Snapshot Biography

Olya Hull was born March 27, 1907, in Rydal, on her grandfather's farm six miles from Belleville. In 1928, in Hebron, Neb., she married Edgar Hull, who died in 1957 at the age of 53. She has one daughter, Nancy Garhart, two granddaughters and three great-grandsons. Years in Kansas: 50.

Caring for Society's Children

Wichita's Carolyn James nurtures the unwanted, abused and handicapped

LPN Eileen Bannister and Carolyn James entertain the children.

Everybody talks about the problems of abused children, crack babies and other children who suffer from their parents' drug addictions. Few do anything about it.

Carolyn James is one exception. For 14 years her arms have been sheltering such children — a total of 18 at last count. She has adopted three severely handicapped children and acts as foster parent to as many as can fit into her four-bedroom Wichita home.

"Nobody else wanted them. I had the education and expertise to help them. Somebody has to do it."

Shasta, the first child Carolyn adopted, had been beaten by her parents when she was two weeks, four weeks and six weeks old. She suffered numerous broken bones and the final beating fractured her tiny skull, leaving her with severe motor damage and no communication.

"She is unable to sit, walk or talk. I met Shasta when I tested her in Garden City as an infant. Then I moved to Wichita to work at Rainbows, and Shasta ended up there, too. She was in foster care and I offered to help the foster parents by taking her for a little while. They said, 'Sure, how about this weekend?' And she became my little girl; I adopted her nine years ago."

When "Hatteberg's People" visited Carolyn James and her children about five years ago, she was in the process of adopting Amanda, a curly-haired baby who was blind and hypersensitive to touch.

"Mandy had genetic problems and her parents asked that she be killed when she was two weeks old. I got her when she was two months and had her until she died in my arms

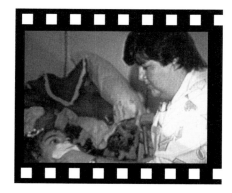

when she was three and a half. Mandy strengthened us in a lot of ways: Her love, smiles, joy, the way she could fight, her orneriness. I'll tell you, her death broke Mommy's heart."

Since then, Carolyn has adopted Neecee, who is autistic and retarded. Neecee came as a foster child three and a half years ago; she is now four. Carolyn has three foster children, all handicapped. They include one who is 10 months older than Shasta and, like Shasta, has a tracheotomy that requires around-the-clock monitoring. A nurse comes at night to keep watch. Carolyn also has a fetal alcohol syndrome baby who has just turned a year old, and a six-year-old who is ambulatory but severely retarded and has behavioral problems.

As if meeting the overwhelming demands of such children weren't enough, Carolyn has dedicated one bedroom of her home to respite care. Multihandicapped children can come to her for a weekend or a few days, giving their beleaguered caregivers a break.

Carolyn James knows the importance of giving herself a break too.

"I have a very good support system, through my church and friends. Every other week I take off, leaving after school and not returning until after midnight, while others look after the kids. Friends and I will go to the theater or take off for Tonkawa for a wild night of bingo. Once a year I take a long holiday. This fall I am going to Montana for 12 days; no children, no responsibilities."

Carolyn was prepared by life and education for her demanding work. As a child, she was struck in the head by a baseball bat, causing her to have severe seizures almost daily. The schools wanted nothing to do with her.

"My parents were told that I would never finish school. They fought to keep me in school, they fought for my rights. That's what probably drove me to want to fight for other children."

Eventually the seizures were controlled by medication. Carolyn not only finished high school, she went on to get a bachelor's in special education at Michigan State University and a master's in elementary education counseling at Wichita State University.

For a year she worked in special education in Michigan, then came to Kansas. She spent five years working for a Garden City special education cooperative. Then she moved to Rainbows United, a Wichita school for the handicapped, where she worked for four years until she took Shasta into her home.

"The good Lord is responsible. When I took Shasta and it became obvious that I could not work at Rainbows and also take care of her, I asked the Lord what I should do. The answer was to quit my job and I said, 'OK Lord'. All this opened up. I had a good deal of faith when I was growing up, and I have acquired a lot more."

The state Social and Rehabilitation Service pays her for the foster care she gives. Although that stops when she adopts a child, SRS foots the formidable medical bills for Shasta and Neecee. Carolyn also is paid for her respite work. Financially, she gets by.

And she and the children live in a house filled with love that emanates from an ever-busy, ever-calm Carolyn, who isn't bitter when she thinks of the horrible damage done to these and other children.

"Oh, I get angry, for instance when Shasta is hurting. I get angry at parents for abusing their children, but then, they usually are drug addicts or were abused children themselves. So I get angry at society. This is a problem that goes from generation to generation. It has to stop somewhere."

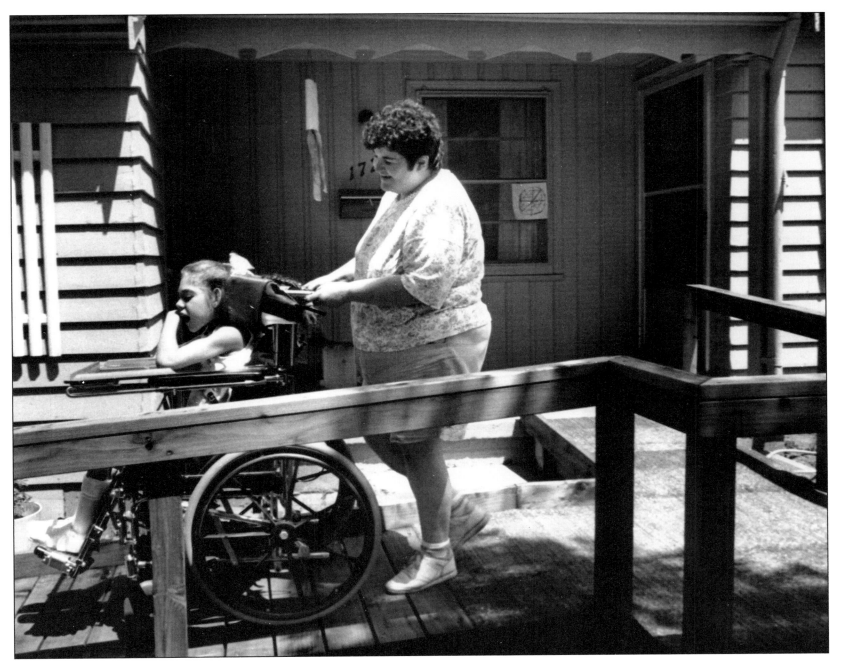

Carolyn James with Shasta on the special ramp outside their house.

Snapshot Biography

Carolyn James was born in California, grew up in the heart of the redwood country and moved several times as a child. She graduated from Crescent City High School and earned a bachelor's from Michigan State University and a master's from Wichita State University. She has two adopted daughters. Years in Kansas: 15.

Ike's Photographer

Eisenhower family, photos form special bond with Abilene's Bill Jeffcoat

There are few people in Abilene, or Kansas for that matter, who know more about Dwight David Eisenhower than Bill Jeffcoat. Jeffcoat's photography studio is intertwined with the Eisenhower family.

Bill's father, Paul, began the photo tradition, taking the famous photo of the Eisenhower family at home in 1926 when Ike was 36 years old (bottom left). Paul was a high school buddy of Ike's brother, Milton.

Bill Jeffcoat recalled when *Life* magazine later wanted that picture.

"They wanted the negative, and we hated to let it go but Dad got the biggest check he ever received for a picture, which was a thousand dollars, and he was on top of the world."

Bill Jeffcoat loves to talk about Ike. He took hundreds of photos of the man, and became an expert on Ike and his career.

A few photos stand out in Jeffcoat's mind.

"Ike was just touring the boyhood home and he came out of the house and just stooped down, saw a flower, picked it up and put it in his lapel, which was quite a touching thing. There was one time I took his picture, where it looks like he's mad, and I got a letter from his son, John, and he said, 'I'm glad you put that one in there because it gave a touch of reality.'"

One of Jeffcoat's most stirring memories of Ike came in 1952, just after Eisenhower had been elected president.

"He came back to Abilene and there was a big parade for him. He was really enjoying coming back and seeing everybody. I still have chills when I watch old TV film of him talking to huge crowds or talking to men in the service."

There have been Jeffcoats in Abilene since just after the Civil War, but Bill is now the last of four generations in the north-central Kansas town known around the world for the president it produced. The Jeffcoat photographic studio, which Bill still occupies, was opened in downtown Abilene in 1921.

Bill went to work for Jeffcoat Studios at age 12, though he didn't decide to become involved in the business as an adult until his mid 20s, after he had graduated from Antioch College in Ohio and spent time in Chicago and New York.

"I came back in 1948. In 1950, the Eisenhower for president thing was starting to warm up. I thought this was the chance of a lifetime to be here."

He met the nation's top photographers and newsmen and watched Edward R. Murrow in action.

"You had a sense of history. You were watching history in the making."

In the 1950s, on Ike's visits back to Abilene, most of Jeffcoat's photos were taken on a Speedgraphic, which used four-by-five-inch negatives — much larger than those of the 35mm, which was just being introduced. In those years, the Jeffcoats got so many requests for photos they retained an agent in New York.

After Eisenhower died in 1969, Jeffcoat felt he had lost a member of the family.

"Ike kind of represented a father image to all of us."

Jeffcoat's photos and expertise remained in

Surrounded by Ike memorabilia, Bill Jeffcoat pages through his Eisenhower books.

demand and in 1990 he published a book of photos, *Dwight D. Eisenhower: Abilene's Favorite Son,* to celebrate the centennial of Ike's birth.

Now 66, Jeffcoat has no plans for retirement. He maintains the studio at 321 Broadway, but these days he can pick and choose the assignments he wants. Some of his copy work is still done on a hundred-year-old camera.

"I'm glad I was here at the right time to take these pictures and just to do what I did. I don't think I'd change a thing. I really don't."

It may be a darkroom that he works in, but it's photographers like Bill Jeffcoat who bring light to our lives through their photographs.

Photograph by Jeffcoat Studio.
Ike on one of his visits back to Abilene.

Bill Jeffcoat holds the portraits his father took of Eisenhower's parents and the old camera used decades ago.

Snapshot Biography

Bill Jeffcoat was born in Abilene in 1925. He attended Abilene High School and Antioch College, Ohio. His wife, Joan, died in 1988. Years in Kansas: 60.

A Farmer Who Doesn't Trust Big Machines

Maple Hill's Howard Johnstone sows memories pulled by horsepower

Some farmers sow corn, wheat or milo. Howard Johnstone of Maple Hill is different. Johnstone sows memories — memories of a simpler time when horsepower was fed by oats and grass.

Johnstone farms with real horsepower, in the form of Belgian horses he breeds and raises.

"I never went out in the morning and saw a little tractor sitting by a big tractor. Horses reproduce, you know."

And, until classification, the horses and the implements they pulled brought in property-tax bills that rarely went over $5 per piece of equipment.

"There was a little feeling towards horse farmers a few years ago. They thought they were kind of dumb. But we're getting a good price for these horses and we're getting the job done and we're not running to the bank with a worried look on our face all the time like the tractor farmer, so it's changed the attitude of some people .... Being old-fashioned's not the worst thing in the world."

Johnstone graduated from Kansas State University in Manhattan in 1943 with a degree in agriculture. He went into the Army and was taken as a prisoner of war by the Germans when they captured Gen. Patton's Third Army shortly before the Battle of the Bulge. He escaped in the spring of 1945 when, with the Russians advancing, the Germans took about 1,500 prisoners out of Poland and back to Germany. He and another man hid in a barn for 32 days, existing only on milk from the cows and turnips they stole from the cows' feed bunks. The experience entrenched his existing appreciation for the basics in life and, surprisingly, did nothing to quench his appetite for turnips — although he says he much prefers the way his wife, Glenna, prepares them.

When he tried to buy a farm in Kansas, bankers were reluctant to lend money to a man who wanted to cultivate the soil with horses, so he and his wife moved to Texas for 10 years. They returned with enough money to buy a farm near Dover. Still, well-meaning friends advised him to buy machinery.

"If I'd taken folks' advice, I'd probably gone broke and had to work at the Goodyear plant. That's happened to a lot of people."

Johnstone farms 240 acres in northeast Kansas. Occasionally, he hires a neighboring farmer to do specialty work for him, but mostly he tends the entire acreage with only his Belgians.

"I'm not too proud to use the big machines. I hope I've got sense enough not to buy any."

In 1982, he described his deep appreciation of horses.

"I had a friend visiting here couple of days ago. We came out here in the morning, and I told him, I said, 'Well, if you had the choice of rolling over in the morning and facing Farrah Fawcett, or coming out here and greeting all these horses,' I said, 'take the horses.' "

His way of life masks the fact that he's a sharp businessman. His is one Kansas farm that makes money. Johnstone sells many of his draft horses, some going for more than $2,500. And, as a sideline, the Johnstones make and market decals, posters and hats with livestock themes at fairs and by mail order.

In 1991, he stopped holding horse sales, but he still had five Belgian geldings he used as draft horses, plus a few mares and colts and a stallion. Those animals should provide the basis for enough horsepower to do all the farming he wants to do.

Howard Johnstone works his team of Belgian draft horses.

"I'm just glad to get along. I just don't have the bankers . . . breathing down my neck all the time, and that's worth a lot. Like I say, I don't make a lot of money, but I don't spend a lot of money."

"Life can be simple if you let it. A lot of people just won't let it."

Snapshot Biography

Howard Johnstone was born Sept. 8, 1922, in Wamego. He married Glenna on April 2, 1948, in Wamego. He earned an agriculture degree from Kansas State University in Manhattan. Years in Kansas: 57.

Mother to More Than 60 Kids

Freda Keck of Auburn opened her door and heart to foster children

Freda in her home of 50 years.

When 90-year-old Freda Keck counts her blessings, there are at least 60. She lives with her poodle Mickey, an adopted stray cat and many, many blessings in a farmhouse on the edge of Auburn, a small town near Topeka.

She moved to the farmhouse exactly half a century ago, but it's never been as quiet as it is now. She and husband Bill had one son of their own, adopted two more children, and 57 others called her "Mom," at least for a while, over a span of 39 years. Freda, who was named for her dad, even named some of the babies, including choosing an appropriate Oriental name for a Japanese baby.

"Some were here several years, until they got through school. I'd just as soon keep them. It was hard to let go."

When their son, Billy, was in his teens, Freda kept her niece's baby for a few months while she was in California. Freda — who had taught hundreds of children in the 1920s in Barton and Shawnee County country schoolhouses — so missed the baby when the niece returned that she decided to board children for the Kansas Children's Service League.

The first of many — Lanie — came to live with them in 1945 when he was barely a year old. He was not placed for adoption because of many health problems, but the Kecks adopted him at the age of 18. Jeannie was still a baby when she came to live with

the Kecks in 1947. She was adopted into the family also, and in 1985 died of cancer, leaving behind two daughters of her own.

At times the Keck house was filled with as many as eight children. Freda was forced to quit taking in children in 1974 after the death of her husband.

Despite the lack of foster children racing down the lane behind the house, Freda's life is still full, just a little quieter. Her four grandchildren and four great-grandchildren live nearby and bring life to the five-bedroom house on the edge of Auburn.

The children's footsteps have long since faded from the steps to the second story — which Freda can no longer visit because of knee surgery — but she fills her time with her pets, her church, her crocheting, her music and writing an occasional poem.

There are those misty moments when Freda thinks about the past. Fortunately, those are few.

"Used to be calves and pigs and geese and chickens and turkeys and that makes me feel bad when I look out and I can't see those things."

For years, she took care of chickens and a goat.

"They were my therapy. You know, I wouldn't go outside at all, if I didn't come out and look out for these chickens."

She still has Mickey, her 9-year-old poodle, however, and a stray cat she affectionately calls Kitty.

"Yeah, I talk to Mickey. I talk to him. Mickey's like a person, really."

And she does go outside: to church, to Bible study, to the Methodist Church for lunch every day, except when the weather's bad and someone brings the meal to her. Unable to walk after many surgeries, family and friends are glad to help her get around. Many have been thanked with one of her handmade afghans.

"Everybody's so good here in Auburn, I couldn't get along otherwise."

She also still plays the organ by ear and takes her portable keyboard with her to the church for lunch on the days her Senior Citizen Kitchen Band rehearses for its area performances at senior centers. While other members of the Senior Citizen Kitchen Band play their pans, washboards and bells, Freda lends the melody with her keyboard.

"Some can hardly stand up. They could prop us up," she says, laughing.

Someone asked Freda once if she'd move to a retirement center. Her answer: "Only if I can take my animals, sewing machine and piano." So Freda still lives at home, the house she moved to 50 years ago, a house that became home to 60 children.

"I hope I stay here as long as I live. I'm happy."

"Everybody's so good here in Auburn, I couldn't get along otherwise."

Snapshot Biography

Freda Keck was born in Brown County, Kan., Jan. 6, 1901. She graduated from Hoisington High School and Emporia State Teachers College. Her husband, William "Bill," died in 1974. They had three children: William Jack "Billy" (born 1930), Lanie (born 1944; adopted at the age of 18); Jeannie (1947-1985; adopted at the age of 10); four grandchildren and four great-grandchildren. Years in Kansas: 90.

Freda with poodle, Mickey, and joyous memories.

Breaking Wild Horses on the Open Plain

Paul and Carl Keith know that a mouthful of dust goes with the territory

Two miles south of Penokee, which is five miles west of Hill City, in the high country of northern Kansas, Paul Keith and his son, Carl, buck the tide of history as they ply the trade of taming horses on the open plain.

"Yeah, we enjoy it—we like it out here," said Paul, who started training and breaking horses full time 15 years ago.

Take the smell of leather, the dry taste of dust, an old dog and a hot Kansas day — couple it with a father-and-son team who love to break horses, and you have the story of the Keith family.

"Well, to my thinking, it's about the top of the line in the horse business," said Paul as he ambled up to the latest prospect for breaking.

Visitors are warned to stay their distance.

"Look out, she may jump right on top of you," Paul said. "There are good ones and bad ones, easy ones and hard ones."

Carl grew up helping his dad taming wild horses. He began taking on responsibilities while in junior high school.

"He'll turn her loose and see if she can buck the saddle off," Carl said. "Dad's always taught me to be careful and pay attention. That's the main thing, you never fall asleep around the colts."

To do this kind of work, you've got to have a lot of patience and horse sense.

"Well, I guess that's the thrill for me: to take something nobody else knows what to do with and make something of it," Paul said.

"I guess if a person is fortunate enough to ride a good horse a time or two . . . like that one,

you get kind of hooked on how he got that way, you know. This horse will bird-dog 'em just like a dog. I can tell within 30 days if they're going to have ability and desire."

There are few who pursue this rugged occupation. It's a hard line of work.

"In the hottest part of the summer, we try to do a lot in the mornings, but you still have to go out in the afternoon," Paul said. "In the winter it's slower, and then when it gets really cold, we call a halt to it. But I still ride the pens at feedyards to check for sick ones."

They are a quiet duo — this father-son team. A team where both are saddled with respect for each other.

"I see other people with kids who can't wait to get gone, so I feel pretty lucky that . . . he's a pretty good kid even if I have to say so," Paul said.

"As far as I'm concerned, nobody can break one any better than him, so who better to learn by than him," said Carl, who adds that college friends are usually surprised when he tells them how he spends his summers.

There are precious moments in all our lives and these are fleeting ones for the Keiths.

"I don't know for sure if I'll be able to come back here with Dad," Carl said.

Carl graduated from Fort Hays State University and is now pursuing his master's degree in mathematics at Kansas State University. He'd like to stay in Penokee. But he's getting married soon, and this type of business is seasonal.

Carl Keith works a horse in the early stages of breaking it in.

But reality is a horse the Keiths can't break. So even as these moments may go by slowly on a summer day, these two very quiet men know these days may not last forever.

"I sure have enjoyed it," Paul said. "He's been helping me a long time."

"I'd stay in a minute if I could," Carl said. "I really enjoy it."

"Well, I guess that's the thrill for me: to take something nobody else knows what to do with and make something of it," Paul said.

Paul Keith at the end of another long day.

Snapshot Biography

Paul Keith was born Jan. 22, 1942, in Penokee. His father was born and raised on the same land. His grandfather came to Kansas from Scotland in the late 1800s. Paul and his wife, JoAnn, were married in 1967. Years in Kansas: 49. Carl was born on Sept. 13, 1968. Carl attended Colby Community College and graduated from Fort Hays State in 1991. Years in Kansas: 23.

Keeper of the Brownings' Legend
Winfield's Philip Kelley walks in footsteps of 19th-century poets

" How do I love thee? Let me count the ways. I love thee to the depth and breadth and height my soul can reach."

While these famous lines are known the world over, it is the life commitment of a Kansan that will illuminate Elizabeth Barrett Browning's work for future generations. The poems and letters of the great Victorian poet have found a home and a friend, not in a world capital or even a large university, but in the unlikely community of Winfield, Kan. Researcher Philip Kelley's ambition for more than two decades has been to print every surviving letter of the Brownings in detail so massive, *The New York Times* called him foolhardy, heroic or both.

"I know more about Elizabeth Barrett Browning than her husband. He didn't even know when she was born . . . that was one of the facts."

Kelley, the former president of the New York Browning Society, spends his days and nights transversing the 19th-century, uncovering letters and tracking down allusions in thousands of letters written by the great English poets Robert Browning and Elizabeth Barrett Browning.

He has walked in their footsteps on Wimpole Street and helped turn their home in Florence, Italy, into a museum, but he chooses to make Kansas the home base for himself and his Wedgestone Press, which so far has published nine volumes of their letters. From his home in Winfield, Kelley travels this country and abroad doing his life's work of compiling all 12,000 letters written by the poets.

He spent more than two decades compiling and editing the collection before the first volume was published; since then about one volume a year has been published. He expects the collection to eventually reach 40 volumes. Not only has he pored over the Brownings' 600 love letters to each other, but also their correspondence to such Victorian figures as Dickens, Carlyle, Tennyson and Wordsworth.

"It's taken me 21 years to find all these, get access to it, make photocopies, get it catalogued and filed."

From 19th-century letters to 20th-century technology, the Browning correspondence is computerized, dated, organized and every allusion explained using a custom-designed computer program. Kelley also has collected some original manuscripts, letters, furniture and a Bernini bust once owned by the Brownings.

"The Brownings owned about 2,5000 books in their own personal library. I have about 6 percent of that library. It is the largest collection of Browning in private hands."

The volumes of letters, which are being distributed by the University of Kansas Press, have received critical acclaim: *The New York Times* Book Review called the collection "brilliantly conceived" and the London Review of Books called it invaluable: "When complete, it will be one of the greatest editions of Victorian correspondence ever produced."

Kelley's interest in the poets originally was piqued while he was a student assistant in the Baylor

Kelley works with co-editor Scott Lewis.

University library, which houses a large Browning collection. After graduation, he set out for London to become an apprentice in the rare book trade. His interest in the Brownings increased after meeting the great-grand nephew of Elizabeth Barrett Browning. In 1961, he received a Guggenheim Fellowship to do a checklist of Browning, and over the years his research has been supported by National Endowment for the Humanities grants.

After six years in London, Kelley moved to New York to edit a diary of Elizabeth Barrett Browning he had found in England. He bought an editorial service in New York City, which eventually was bought by *The New York Times,* and in 1978 he decided to move back to his home state.

Kelley makes the transition easily from Winfield to Harvard, Yale, Princeton, the Library of Congress or abroad, where he spends up to six months of the year. There are differences in lifestyle, but they matter little to the man who has not gone to the movies since 1956 and who spends at least 85 hours a week consumed by life in another era.

"The Brownings are a thread that has given me an exciting life. I'm so excited by what I'm doing on a daily basis I have no need for escape."

Snapshot Biography

Philip Kelley was born Dec. 19, 1934, in Arkansas City. He graduated from Baylor University with an English degree in 1961. Years in Kansas: 29.

Kansas' Most Prolific Sci-Fi Writer

Karen Lee Killough of Manhattan has seen Topeka in the 21st century

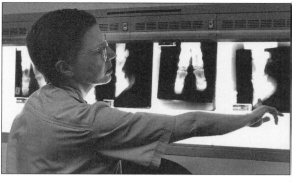

Books can transport us to anywhere in the world – or in the universe, for that matter. And oftentimes it's someone you wouldn't suspect whose writing can do the transporting. That's the case with Karen Lee Killough, one of Kansas' most successful science fiction writers.

"Everybody I meet at work says, 'You're an author. You're famous.' Ah, you know . . . they're thrilled."

They should be. Karen Killough is a gifted writer of science fiction and mystery novels. She's published 11 books.

But her readers might be surprised to know that this writer works by day in a white uniform as chief technologist in radiology at Kansas State University's School of Veterinary Medicine in Manhattan.

In the radiology lab, there's talk of X-rays, graphs and ultra-sound tests. It's a high-tech job with some risk – that's why she's on crutches. While X-raying a horse, it fell on her.

"He was needle shy and when they stuck him with the needle in order to tranquilize him, he lost his balance and fell. I ran, but not fast enough or far enough. He landed on top of me when he fell."

Despite the injury, Karen says her job helps her with her science fiction writing, especially when she's trying to describe aliens.

"Knowing alternative anatomy has sometimes given me ways to set up aliens. I have to know how I can attach that extra set of limbs logically and get away with it."

From horses to aliens, Karen's mind can reach past the limits of the K-State vet school to the outer limits of the universe to write such books as *Deadly Silents* or *A Voice Out of Ramah*. As a radiology technologist she works with facts she can't change. But in her literary world, she is in complete control.

"Maybe it's just the fact that you can be Lord of your own world. . . you can be a world builder or a world destroyer and you can make everybody do what you want them to do because they are your people."

One of the hardest parts for any writing is putting what's in the brain down on paper so the reader sees the same image.

"I know what I want to do but sometimes finding the right words is difficult. But with the computer you can keep changing your mind. You can find yourself re-writing ad infinitum. . . . Sometimes there are too many choices."

Though her formal training is as a radiology technologist, Karen has always had a desire to write. Her father was an English teacher and her mother worked for a newspaper in Atchison.

"When I was 4 years old, I used to make up TV and radio episodes, and I always had a fascination with language."

Although she was involved in a writers' group, Karen says she "basically" taught herself how to write.

Her husband, an attorney, talked her into writing short stories in the 1970s because she kept talking about doing it someday.

Karen writes under the name Lee Killough – Lee is her middle name – because she "likes the alliteration better." Friends and co-workers have been impressed, which is a relief.

"My colleagues are fascinated and amazed at my books, which is nice because it (science fiction writing) used to be looked on askance."

Killough (above) examines X-rays as part of her duties at KSU. Below, she relaxes with one of her equine patients.

Some of her novels include *Spider Play*, *Doppelganger Gambit*, and *Dragon's Teeth*. All three are murder mysteries set in Topeka in the 21st century.

Karen's books are published under the Quarter imprint, owned by Warner Books. Two of her early works were vampire novels set in Kansas: *Blood Hunt* and *Bloodlines*. Another fantasy novel is set in Africa.

Her husband, Howard, who is now retired due to a nervous degenerative disease, is also a writer. In the late 1980s, he wrote a book on copyrights that has gone through several printings.

While Karen Killough writes about other worlds, her own life combines the world of animals, the reality of teaching and the fantasy of science fiction. And it is that fantasy that sets her apart.

"As one of my students said, I'm not just another one of the techs that bosses them around. I'm somebody."

Snapshot Biography

Karen Lee Killough was born May 5, 1942, in Syracuse. She grew up in Atchison and graduated from Atchison High School in 1960. She attended Fort Hays State University for two years, and then enrolled in the radiology technology program at Hadley Memorial Hospital in Hays. She worked at hospitals in Concordia and Manhattan, then moved to Washingon, D.C., where she lived for two years while her husband was stationed at Andrews Air Force Base. She has lived in Manhattan since 1970 and has worked for the Kansas State University School of Veterinary Medicine since 1971. She and her husband, Howard Patrick Killough, have been married since 1966. Years in Kansas: 47.

A Grandma Who Makes Circuit Boards

Betty Koop of Wichita takes on high tech with a high spirit

The new Air Force One built at Boeing, the revolutionary Voyager aircraft that flew around the world and the specialized circuitry used in other space-age vehicles – all benefited from the sight and touch of 80-year-old Betty Koop.

Betty, working in the basement of her Wichita home, had a part in the construction and success of those planes because she decided two decades ago to go back to work.

Her work making circuit boards is intricate. The number of people who have the skill and experience to successfully make the tiny boards is so small that aircraft companies seek her out for jobs. And they are perfectly content to let her set her own hours and work at home.

"I just keep a-going . . . . My kids are really amazed at me."

Betty is one of those amazing ageless people whose life isn't a stereotype.

Eighteen years ago, following the death of her husband, Betty Koop continued his side business of making exotic circuit boards for companies which brought her the designs.

Making the circuit boards requires a magnifying eyepiece and is a 15-step process. A small drill with miniature bits etches the circuits onto a negative.

Betty's life is full and constantly moving. When not making circuit boards, she might be busy on another one of her hobbies – photography, and traveling when she can. She's more than glad to show you the photograph she took of the Eiffel Tower.

She is also a student of genealogy, loves history and enjoys cooking.

Always on the move, she has been involved in volunteer civil defense organizations, the Red Cross and scouting organizations. Betty isn't one to slow down now.

She is still involved with the American Historical Society, which is devoted to those with German or Russian heritage, and is writing her life story. Her 80th birthday party was attended by 86 friends and family members.

"My family wants me to publish my poetry. They're real proud of me, I guess. I like to keep active. It keeps me younger."

Betty is a woman who lives and loves life, but it is in her poetry that her sensitivity is truly expressed. Her poems speak to the heart of good memories back on the farm and of difficult times.

"Sometimes I just write a poem in my head. Next day I write it down and go back and drill some more. I get sentimental sometimes."

Eric is a grandson who died several years ago. Her poems echo a grandmother's heartbreak.

"My heart aches when I think of Eric,
Eric with laughing blue eyes.

His happy 'Hi, Grandma' –
I miss him so . . .

My heart cries, and cries . . . and cries."

And there are pleasant memories from life seven decades ago on a farm near Halstead, in a poem titled "The Sounds of Summer":

"The golden glow of the sunset low in the western sky,
brings back to me sweet memories of happy days gone by.

The farm on a cool summer evening, the smell of new-mown hay,
the sound of happy voices of children at play.

The lowing of the cattle as they settle for the night,
the changing colors in the sky as the sun sinks out of sight.

The pigeons in the hayloft cooing to their young,
Dad's tractor in the distance, how steady is the hum.

The smell of fresh-baked bread, our mother's lovely face,
the memory of the songs she sang, that time cannot erase.

Betty gets ready to apply the drill to make the finite circuitry.

The hoot owl in the cottonwood such a lonely haunting tune,
the beauty of the starlit sky, the brilliant silver moon.

The quiet of the evening wind whispering through the trees,
the lovely sounds of summer – Oh, how I cherish these.

The shadow of the red barn, the old house with its charm,
it's so pleasant to remember, those childhood years spent on the farm."

Betty is in touch with her feelings and in touch with life, whether she's concentrating on the 20th-century technology in her basement or on family and friends.

"I want to live my life so someone will miss me when I'm gone. I really enjoy everything in life and I want to live to be a hundred."

"I want to live my life so someone will miss me when I'm gone."

Snapshot Biography

Betty Koop was born on May 17, 1911, on a farm near Halstead. She attended Mount Hope High School. She and her husband, Arthur, were married on Sept. 24, 1933, and moved to Wichita in 1938. Her husband died in 1973. She has three daughters, Marilyn of Omaha, Lillian of Wichita, and Linda of Racine, Wis.; a son, Kelly of Dallas, and six grandchildren. Years in Kansas: 80.

Betty Koop with stories she has written for her grandchildren.

Going for the Gold in Tae-Kwon-Do

Shawna Larson hopes to give Arkansas City worldwide attention in '92

She's a young Olympic hopeful and her eyes are set on Barcelona, Spain, for 1992. And there's a good chance that the entire sports world will get to know more about Arkansas City through the Tae-Kwon-Do skills of Shawna Larson.

A senior at Arkansas City High School, 17-year-old Shawna has been studying the art of Tae-Kwon-Do since she was 8 years old. Shawna got into Tae-Kwon-Do after her brother, Jesse, became involved. Today, she is considered an expert in the Korean martial arts system which is similar to karate.

The young Olympic hopeful has already made a number of sports headlines by winning national competitions, beating contestants a decade older. Shawna is not shy about why she works so hard at this unusual sport or in sharing her dreams.

"Winning, I like to win."

Shawna Larson is one of the best Tae-Kwon-Do fighters in the United States.

In 1990, she made the U.S. Olympic team and trained during the summer in Colorado Springs at the Olympic Training Center. Her goal is to compete in the 1992 Olympics in Barcelona.

"I have a goal and this is my dream and so I want to go to '92 and I want to make it."

In the summer of 1990, Shawna trained 6 1/2 hours a day at the training center.

"During the school year, I try to train six times a week. So I like to keep it 2 1/2 to 3 hours a day."

She is like any young woman with a dream. Mixing her Tae-Kwon-Do career with school requires a delicate balancing act.

When she's not studying, playing softball or practicing Tae-Kwon-Do, there's still time to be on the pom-pon squad at school, play tennis and work part time as a waitress.

"I don't think anything is too hard if you want to learn and you set your mind to it."

Shawna travels all over the world winning gold medals. But this year Shawna has taken a different direction in her training. Rather than be constantly on the go and at risk for an injury that would keep her out of the trials next year, she and her parents, Jack and Linda Larson, made the decision that she should stay in Arkansas City and train.

Though Shawna is calm when talking about her athletic accomplishments to date, that calm betrays the power Shawna displays during tournaments. She's aggressive and intense in competition.

"When you go to competitions, you feel real good; this is what you trained for and you have to show them what you can do.

"I don't know what I would do if at this point they said no more Tae-Kwon-Do. I don't know what I would do."

Still, the hours, the heat and the pain are worth the effort. Her sport has been a passport to the world. She has been in tournaments in Korea and Taiwan, the World Cup in Madrid and the Pan Am Games in Puerto Rico.

"I don't think anything is too hard if you want to learn and you set your mind to it."

And Shawna has certainly proven that. At the age of 9, she won her first competition. It was in 1990 in Madison, Wis., where she competed against athletes in their late 20s and early 30s and won a gold medal in the senior nationals.

Shawna has won two gold medals in junior nationals, but will compete next year at the senior level in the sport, which will be a part of the Olympics as a demonstration sport.

Her coach and trainer is Primo Venegas of Kim's Academy. Venegas trains under Joon Y. Kim of Kim's Academy in Wichita. Kim, who also has worked with Shawna, said he believes her chances next year are very good.

To be a winner, Shawna says these are the priorities she tries to apply to her sport:

"Self-confidence, discipline, integrity, and have the ability to concentrate and focus your mind on one thing."

Other teenagers sometimes kid her about her sport, especially the boys.

"But you get some of the guys going around and saying, 'Hey karate woman,' making kung fu sounds and stuff like that. Or sometimes they say, 'We don't have to worry if we get in trouble, she'll take care of us.'"

She takes the kidding in stride. But in competition, this teenager isn't kidding.

"I don't feel it is a violent sport. I don't think anything can stop me now."

climbing to top in taekwondo

Snapshot Biography

Shawna Larson was born on Feb. 24, 1974, in Arkansas City. She will graduate from high school there in 1992. Her parents are Jack and Linda Larson, and she has a brother, Jesse, 22, who attends the University of Kansas. Years in Kansas: 17.

The Oldest Reporter in the Country
Rose Nix Leo of Howard wants to die with pen in hand

Rose Leo of Howard has been writing for newspapers for around 70 years. She's not about to let a broken wrist, three compressed spinal disks and other injuries stop her. So shortly after she banged herself up in a fall at her home July 29, 1991, she was back to submitting her news items and farm reminiscences to the *Elk County Citizen-Advance News* in Howard.

"I've still got this arm," she said, pointing to her uninjured right arm, "and I've still got this brain. Of course I'm still writing. No. I'm not retired."

The woman with the short white hair and the rosy, weathered face was born April 30, 1894, in a claim house near Norman, Okla. After her parents died one after the other, Rose Nix, age 8, and her younger brother, Tom, came to Severy to be reared by her father's aunt. She has lived in southeast Kansas since.

"I always liked to write, and I started about 70 years ago writing local news wherever I lived."

She moved into Howard from the farm in 1969 and started gathering news: who was born, who died, who's sick, who has visitors or is visiting, who has a new coonhound. She spends all day Monday and half a day Tuesday tramping sturdily around Howard, asking for news items. Then she goes home and writes her gleanings on the back of used computer paper. She didn't consider herself extraordinary until the *Detroit Free Press* launched a nationwide search for the oldest living reporter.

"They thought maybe they would find people 65. I was 93 at the time. I won for the whole United States. A reporter, Gary Blonston, came to town and interviewed me and the story went all over. I've been interviewed 23 times in my home. I was on Dan Rather's 'CBS News' and KAKE's 'Hatteberg's People.' "

The stories have created dozens of admiring fans who write letters or make telephone calls from all over the United States and Canada.

"You're an inspiration! That's what's said to me more than any other words."

From her prodigious memory comes another column, "From the Farm," which she has been writing

for about three years and which appears in five area weeklies. It's her memory of farm life, dating back to her girlhood in Oklahoma and Kansas.

"There was an ad in the paper saying they wanted stories of old country living. I sent a story about running the binder in the field. The editor said, "Write more."

In 1989, she suffered a broken rib. A friend, Mary Perkins, while giving her back rubs urged Rose to pull her columns together in a book. At first, Rose resisted, but soon she was enthusiastic and in 1990 she published a thick volume, *Rose's Last Scrap*.

She drew the name from the "Last Scrap," which she calls the little paragraphs, often inspirational, that conclude her newspaper columns. In the first paragraph of the book, she explained that the title comes from the Gospel of John, where Jesus tells the disciples to gather every last scrap after he fed the multitudes.

"So I gather up the scraps of endurance, trust, forgiveness, love, forbearance, any and all morsels of worth, expanding on them, that by my words you may be encouraged and feel a sense of pleasure and comfort."

Rose has called on all those "morsels of worth" to help her through a long life that has had more than its share of tribulation and challenges.

"I don't know why, but I thought it was a disgrace to be an orphan."

When she and her younger brother came to Severy their 60-year-old great aunt said she would take one of the children, and asked Rose's great uncle which of the children he would take. He responded brusquely, "I don't want either of them." There still is pain, nearly 90 years later, in remembering that rejection. The aunt took both of them and raised them on her farm.

"I know my aunt loved me, but she never told me so, she never hugged me. I think that's why I always hugged the children I taught, and why I hug everybody today. I just love people."

But the little girl had lots of friends, and according to her book, an interesting and full life on the farm, where she would tackle any job with relish.

Rose loved children and wanted to be a teacher. She made it through only one year of high school and later took correspondence studies. She substituted for half a year, then taught for six years in rural schools in the Severy area. In an era when marriage usually cost a woman teacher her job, she taught a year after she married John Leo of Elk County in 1920. In tribute to her ability, the school board offered to build them a house on the grounds if she would agree to stay another five years.

"My husband said no, and I let him have his way. But I taught Sunday school and we had three wonderful children; I taught them before they went to school."

Rose now lives alone and, when not sidelined with injuries, takes care of her house, cultivates the garden and cans its bounty, mows the lawn and even washes and irons a neighbor's good shirts because she isn't satisfied with the way a laundry does them.

She volunteers at the senior center. She weaves rugs. She loves to play cards. She is very active in church, helps the Red Cross, is public relations chairman for seven organizations and has been known to visit three cemeteries on Memorial Day to put red poppies on veterans' graves.

"I've always loved to write. I want to be busy and I want my pen in my hand until the last day. I can't quit now. I've got some more things to write."

Snapshot Biography

Rose Leo was born April 30, 1894, near Norman, Okla. Her parents died soon after and she moved to Kansas to be reared by a great aunt. She married John in 1920 and they had a daughter, Anita, and two sons, Frank and Chios, who died in 1953. John died in 1967. She has seven grandchildren, 15 great-grandchildren and four great-great-grandchildren. Years in Kansas: 89.

Rose with her news mailbox, just outside the post office.

"I hope that my mind does not stop stretching or that my soul ceases growing. Even in the golden years, I hope I can live a few moments each day on tiptoe, enchanted by the love of the hills of time."

From the writings of Rose Leo.

Rose Leo gets a hug from Norma Allen in the county Appraiser's office in Howard.

An Ambassador for the 19th Century
Marie MacDonald of Wichita helps folks understand life in a cowtown

She's an ambassador for Old Cowtown Museum, the living museum nestled against the Arkansas River near downtown Wichita. On dusty roads walked hundreds of years ago by Wichitans who lived on the wilder side of life, Marie MacDonald's characters spring to life.

Among the characters Marie portrays are Victoria Murdock, wife of *Wichita Eagle* founder Marcellus Murdock; Rea Anna Woodman, an early day teacher whose husband was one of the booming city's first bankers; and Julia Munger, wife of Darius Munger and one of Wichita's founders. Julia led a busy life, splitting her time running the Munger Hotel, raising her two daughters and being active in social circles.

Marie enjoys portraying Victoria Murdock and Rea Anna Woodman the most.

"Julia is more difficult . . . She had a poker face and hardly ever smiled. . . .

"There is very little written on the early Wichita woman. To do Julia Munger, it took six months of research and two to four months to write it, rewrite it and cut it to a 30-minute performance."

Marie likes to get the characters down so the audience can "really hear the person talk." The characters talk of bearing eight children and losing five, of growing up without a mother, and of the emotion, anger, joy and frustration of a day in the life of a Wichita pioneer woman.

"You try to get people to feel it, to sort of get the psychology into it."

Marie and her husband, Mac, first came to Wichita in the early '40s. They were actors in a touring melodrama production.

"What impressed my husband and me when we came here was the warmth of the people."

Their touring show was a Gay nineties' melodrama that was performed on the roof garden of the Broadview Hotel.

When the war and hard times hit, the acting group disbanded, and the MacDonalds chose to return to Wichita to live.

"People just kind of took us under their wings."

Marie was used to hard times. She had worked for 20 cents an hour in her teens as a telephone company operator. She met Mac when his touring repertory show came to her hometown in the 1930s.

In the late 1940s, Marie got a job working on the *Wichita Eagle's* society pages, but after a year and a half moved to the *Beacon* as society editor in 1950.

"I always wanted to write."

Her career moved into radio at KFBI, where she was director of women's programming for 7 1/2 years. Then she moved on to KARD-TV and later KFH as assistant programming director.

In those years, she refined her interview style and had the opportunity to meet and interview a rising Hollywood star, Ronald Reagan. She also interviewed Bob Hope, Dorothy Lamour and a number of other showbiz and fashion celebrities.

In 1965, she went back to work at the *Eagle* as a feature writer, a position she had for 10 years. It was a job she found both challenging and exciting.

"It was a lot better than when I first worked there, and we used to work 50 to 60 hours and get $25 a week."

She won a National Press Women's competition for a series on the anguish, tension and frustration expressed by wives of American soldiers who visited their husbands in Hawaii, where the soldiers would go for a brief "R&R" – rest and relaxation – trip before heading back to the Vietnam War.

Today, Marie is involved in her church, and continues to write her two columns for the senior citizen newspaper *Active Aging*: a retirees' column and one of her own reflections called "Marie's Moments."

She is an 81-year-old full of young ideas, and through her writing is still commanding an audience.

"They write to me because I'm a stranger and they tell me things that they probably wouldn't have told their best friend."

Ideas for her column flow from an active mind and a porch swing.

"If I am honest about it, I'm usually churning up thoughts for the next column."

She writes the columns in longhand, then types them at the electric typewriter.

As Marie prepared to retire from her newspaper career, an acquaintance at the *Eagle* mentioned that Cowtown was looking for someone with theatrical background to portray early Wichita women. For Marie, it was an opportunity almost too good to be true.

"What is it they say? 'You have to be careful what you wish for because it's liable to come true.' That's the way I felt."

Marie got the job, and has been an ambassador for Cowtown ever since. She makes appearances throughout south-central Kansas. Part of her responsibilities include working with schoolchildren who visit Cowtown, showing them 19th-century items.

"You know what some of the other children thought it was . . . some of the others thought it was a music box. Would you like to come up and grind some coffee?"

The kids help keep her young, Marie says.

"I like working with older people, but I do enjoy the children. I've enjoyed my work at Cowtown so much."

Snapshot Biography

Marie MacDonald was born in Ozark, Ark., on June 1, 1910. She and her husband, King R. "Mac" MacDonald, were married in 1931 and moved in 1942 to Wichita, a city they had been introduced to during a touring stage production. Her husband died in 1966. She has three step-daughters, Marian of Whittier, Calif., Dorothy of Sunnyvale, Calif., and Mollie of Sun City, Ariz. Years in Kansas: 49.

Marie MacDonald wears the special dress that was custom-made to portray as accurately as possible what pioneer women in Wichita wore 100 years ago.

Photo courtesy of Marie MacDonald.

Ronald Reagan visited with Marie MacDonald in Wichita when Reagan was a spokesperson for General Electric in the late 1950s and Marie worked for KARD-TV.

She Sings from the Heart

Phyllis Macy-Mills of Cedar Vale pursues city medicine and country melodies

Carl and Phyllis walk in the rolling hills near Cedar Vale.

Phyllis Macy-Mills of Cedar Vale heals physical wounds by day at the Galachia Medical Group clinic in Wichita. Other times, she addresses the spirit with her poetry set to music. Music about Kansas and its people.

The lyrics are filled with the imagery of the rolling plains and the friendly people who typify the state. Her life as a rancher's wife gives her first-hand experience with cowboys and the rural life her songs often portray.

She rides pastures with her husband, Carl, on their ranch near Cedar Vale in southeast Kansas, about 10 miles north of the Oklahoma border. When they drive across the ranch, Carl knows just where she wants to be let out of the pickup and at what spot she wants to be picked up:

"There's a place in the middle of the ranch where you can look in any direction and not see anything man-made. There's a canyon there that just runs on forever . . . ."

Carl picks her up at the foot of the mile-long canyon.

Phyllis sometimes extends her country outlook to her work at the clinic, which specializes in cardiology, neurology and pulmonology. As a physician's assistant, she recognizes that sometimes all the patient needs is bucket-calf therapy. Get a bucket calf, she tells them. The calf must be fed morning and night; it needs to be cared for and her patient needs to be needed.

"Right now, I have the best of both worlds . . . It's really true."

She also has the support of her friends and the doctors and her co-workers at the clinic.

"They want you to extend yourself as far as you can and challenge yourself. Anybody can do anything they want to do if they think they're big enough to do it."

Phyllis decided to extend herself from writing songs to writing a book. *The Last of the Handshake Cowboys*, her first novel, is based on a song she had written earlier.

"It's a lustful historical western novel set in the early 1900s on the Oklahoma-Kansas border. It has a lot to do with ranching."

Coming from Phyllis Macy-Mills, that is no surprise at all. Kansas and cowboys run through her blood and into her books and the songs she has recorded.

From the original "Handshake Cowboys" song come these words that go to the essence of the character of the people who helped build the state:

"He'd stand there and look you straight in the eye,
And in the set of the jaw you could read,
For the word of the handshake cowboy,
Was all that you'd ever need. . . ."

And her songs on Kansas tell us much about the land:

"Across this open prairie, rolls Kansas far and wide,
Surrounded now by wheat fields, where cowboys used to ride.
And many a cattle trail would lead down these still wide-open plains.
And the air so clear on a given day, you can see for many a mile.
And coming home to Kansas is like the warmth of your best friend's smile."

"There's a place in the middle of the ranch where you can look in any direction and not see anything man-made. There's a canyon there that just runs on forever . . . ."

Snapshot Biography

Phyllis Macy-Mills was born Oct. 8, 1937, in Kingman County. She attended Pratt Community College, earned a bachelor of health science degree from Wichita State University, completed the physician's assistant program at WSU, and did graduate work at the University of Utah. She married Bill Messenger in 1955 in Kingman County. Phyllis has four children. She married Carl Mills on May 2, 1980. Years in Kansas: 54.

Sharing Thoughts with Identical Twin
For Hazel and Hildred, the telephone is just an extra step

Hazel, left, and Hildred, right, looking at Fruit Fresh recipes.

Hazel Manley lives with her husband in Wellington. Her identical twin, Hildred McCammon, lives in Freedom, Okla. At 83 years of age, their resemblance still is uncanny. Also uncanny is the way that their thoughts, even miles apart, are so often identical.

"Half the time when I'm trying to call her she's got the line tied up calling me from Freedom, Okla.," Hazel said. "Or when we put a card in the mail, nine times out of 10 it will be the same card I've bought up here. If we're sending a card to our nieces or nephews, it might be the same card . . . and we've done that many a time for Mother's Day. Same card! When we're together we always dress alike. Lots of times I'll go down to see her and she'll have the same thing I have on."

The twins – born Hazel and Hildred McCammon on Jan. 29, 1907 – were not always that close. For the first seven years of their lives, Hazel said the pair fought incessantly. Then, after a particularly bitter battle, their father came in from the field and settled the issue.

"He had an old razor strap hanging by the door. He hit me once with it and he hit Hildred once with it and he said, 'Now Hildred, you kiss Hazel and promise not to hit and bite and fight anymore,' and he made me do the same thing and we never did fight after that. We had a great time."

They did the usual things that twins do, like tricking family and friends by pretending to be each other, and unwittingly performed similarly in school. Hazel believes that was because the pair studied together, but their teachers were not too sure.

"Our teachers usually sat one in the front of

the room and one in the back of the room. Our history teacher still couldn't believe we wrote the same things. He said, 'I do believe you girls have cheated on the test.'"*

They hadn't, of course, and they didn't always think alike. Hildred, for instance, had used a fruit-preserving product since 1931 because members of her home extension unit had recommended it. She hadn't thought to tell Hazel about it. But when the People Finders agency in New York City found Hazel and Hildred through a national organization for twins, Hazel quickly was introduced to Fruit Fresh. The Fruit Fresh company had asked the agency to find 10 sets of elderly identical twins to interview; one set would be chosen to be in Fruit Fresh advertisements.

"We already knew seven sets who tried out for it. We'd been to so many twins conventions, in Canada and everywhere."

The company chose Hazel and Hildred, and for three years–1988 through 1990–viewers watched the pair tout the merits of Fruit Fresh on television. Celebrity status was not new to Hazel and Hildred. They had appeared in 1980 on the "David Letterman Show" and earned an all-expenses-paid trip to New York, plus $100 each for new dresses. Schoolchildren asked for, and received, autographs and Hazel became an ardent voice for Fruit Fresh.

Now, not only do they buy the same things at the grocery store, but the twins larger purchases remain amazing coincidences as well.

"We went down to Hildred's one time and she had bought a brand new television. Well, it was just exactly like the new one we bought. We didn't either one know the other was going to buy a television. Same with the car one time."

The twins even chose the same career. Both took tests to become certified as teachers and attended classes in Emporia, Wichita, Lawrence, Winfield and Manhattan before accumulating enough credit hours to qualify for their degrees.

"We got a scattering of education all over the country."

Neither of the women had children, and Hildred married a twin, though Hazel did not. Hildred explained:

"She already had her George picked out when I met him," Hildred said. "I was three years too late."

The twins both suffered heart attacks in 1987, but they deviated again from their parallel lives in 1990, when Hazel suffered a heart attack as she was rolling up Hildred's hair for a home permanent. Hildred recalled the incident:

"We'd already gotten her permanent in and were working on mine. The doctors thought that was something. I took Hazel to the hospital with part of my hair rolled up."

One year later, Hazel still tires easily and has to lie down to rest more often than she wanted to. She seemed confident, though, that with a bit more time she would recover completely. She planned to follow her doctor's orders and be patient.

"You take things as they come and as they go. Take it for granted, it's going to happen that way."

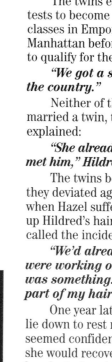

Hildred McCammon, left, Hazel Manley ,right.

Snapshot Biography

Hazel and Hildred McCammon were born Jan. 29, 1907, on a farm southwest of Conway Springs. Hazel graduated from Wellington High School and attended Southwestern College, Winfield. She married George T. Manley on June 30, 1933. Years in Kansas: 84. Hildred also graduated from Wellington High School, then married Wilford McCammon, who happened to have the same last name, in 1936. They have lived in Freedom, Okla., since then. Years in Kansas: 29.

The Train Man of Southeast Kansas

Pittsburg's Johnnie Marietta has tons of fun as a big-time collector

People collect a lot of strange things: stamps, barbed wire, yarn. You name it, and it's collected. But how many people collect railroad cars — from full-sized trains, that is.

Johnnie Marietta of Pittsburg is working on the railroad in his own backyard, and those real train cars are all part of his collection.

"I don't know why I ever started collecting railroad cars — they weigh 90 tons — when I could be collecting postage stamps."

Well, the reason he does it is simple. Johnnie loves everything about trains – so much so that he's got four 90-ton cars sitting in his backyard, and they're all refurbished. He's owned a total of seven, as well as a depot.

"It's always work to keep them up, to keep them in shape. Now I've got to repaint these cars again, and it's a very big job. Sometimes I get awful tired but I fool with them all the time. I live railroad every day, every day."

Johnnie, the son of Italian immigrants, grew up in a coal-mining area in Cherokee County and, when he was old enough, he too went to work in the mines. There, he devised a logo he called "Bozo Texino," a little figure wearing a hat that he drew onto each rail car load of coal leaving the mine. And the urge to draw lingers.

"I still do it, oh hell yes, if I got a piece of soapstone with me."

Sometimes, when he travels, he goes down to railroad yards just to watch the trains come and go, and to read the insignias and inspect the wheels. He travels by train when he can, and by car and camper when he can't.

"I'd rather watch a train go by than watch Notre Dame play football."

Unlike other drivers, Johnnie delights in approaching a railway crossing when the red lights begin to flash and the signal arms drop to block the road.

"I'm always glad to go someplace where the crossing is blocked because a train is going by."

In August 1991, he had just returned from a jaunt to Las Vegas, where he toured Buffalo Bill Cody's private railroad car with the man who had put about $1 million into restoring it. Also in 1991 he was contacted by Boxcar Willie, who wanted to purchase part of Johnnie's collection.

"I was in Gallup, N.M., last month. I met every train for seven days. It was a lot of fun."

His penchant for trains has brought him into contact with a variety of celebrities and railroad people – Ernest Borgnine, Dick Van Dyke, Barbara Mandrell and Mike Haverty, former president of the Santa Fe Railway. "He's been in my house many times. He's a good friend of mine."

Johnnie misses the days, though, when he could go down to the depot at Pittsburg and just watch the trains go by.

"Yeah, I miss it very, very much. It's very sickening to me to see it all gone. I bought

the last ticket that was ever bought out of this depot here."

And then he bought the depot. But then, as with other parts of his collection, he sold it. Now, the depot's been torn down.

Johnnie worries that he is getting too old, at almost 79, to maintain the dining car and cabooses he already owns and has restored.

And it's another passion – the circus – that takes up a lot of his time these days. Johnnie has been invited for the past 10 years to ride in the Great Circus Parade in Milwaukee, Wis. He travels around the country, meeting up with the Ringling Brothers Circus at the best possible places – the railroad stations that carry carloads of animals and equipment.

Whether Johnnie is in his caboose, his passenger car or just flirting with past memories, it's a safe bet that he's thinking about trains or the circuses that travel on them.

"Everybody knows it. They call me 'Crazy Railroad Man' or 'Circus Man.' If you split my head wide open, all you'd see is circus and trains."

Snapshot Biography

Johnnie Marietta was born May 17, 1913, southwest of Cherokee in Cherokee County. He attended the county's Humble School until the eighth grade, when he quit and went to work. He married Helen Calloway "42 or 43 years ago." They are the parents of two sons and two daughters and have six grandchildren. Years in Kansas: 78.

The Woodcarver-Philosopher

Rusty Mauk of Augusta shapes wood and philosophy into an art form

Meet Rusty Mauk: woodcarver, philosopher and just plain good old boy. Rusty has lived in Augusta most of his life. He's been carving wood for 72 years — since he was 6 years old — with everything from knives to little hatchets and axes. His hands show the wear of woodcarving.

"I don't think my hands have ever healed up. They're always smashed or cut up or something. But at least I've got all my fingers."

Rusty, who was born in a sod house on a Cherokee Indian Reservation in Oklahoma, is one of a handful of carvers who make totem poles. He also makes wooden Indians and shared his secret for carving those.

"What you do is take a log and cut off everything that doesn't look like an Indian."

Rusty loves a good joke, likes people and mixes his work with his talk. He kept up a steady patter as he chipped away at a log, searching for the eagle he knew was hidden inside.

"Oh, it's just a pastime, it's good for what ails a guy. It's just like a mean woman. When she's mean, you can get out of the house and go to wood carving, you know that? It's not long before she'll be down talking to you again, you know that? Yeah, that's just kind of the way it goes."

Some of Rusty's carvings weigh more than 500 pounds, and each has its own distinct personality. A few are made from "pretty white wood" that "looks about like a school marm's leg." Some are carved with meticulous attention to detail and others, like a pioneer woman he was displaying several years ago, are "pretty" only in an early frontier sort of way.

"One of the gals who walked across with the wagon train, that's who that's patterned after. She's got kind of a pretty face, though, hasn't she?"

The person who bought her must have thought she did. Buyers for his carvings, in fact, are plentiful. His work is sent around the country, and people come to his home in Augusta to choose from the carvings there.

"I'll make 'em fit your pocketbook. If you've got any money, I'll get it. I give a lot of these away, but then I found out you get money for it so I went to doing it for money. You know it makes a difference. . . . Yeah, you don't have any trouble getting rid of them. There's always some sucker that'll buy them, you know that?

"One guy came from New Jersey. He liked one and then he liked a bunch of others. He just rented a U-Haul truck and hired somebody to drive it back."

Rusty estimates he's about a year behind on orders, but he refuses to hurry to meet the demand. He has other interests, like steam and gas engines, that have taken up his time since he retired after 30 years as a machine tooler and electronics engineer at Boeing in Wichita. There's no welding shop in his area, so he sandwiches welding for friends and neighbors into his schedule, too. He also takes time to teach other people how to carve wood.

"I just kind of whittle when I take a notion to. . . . I just kind of like to do it in my spare time. I'd hate to be a woodcarver, though; I'd rather just do it when I wanted to do it. I think you're better at it."

Rusty's carvings from solid pieces of wood are classics, and so is Rusty. Success hasn't changed him a whit, from the tip of his boots to the top of the battered, sweat-and-oil-soaked hat he always wears.

"Well that hat, I bought it in 1928 in Denver, Colorado, at the Farmer and Stockman at 15th and Laramie. I paid seven dollars and 35 cents

for it. My wife thinks I ought to get the oil changed in it, but it's a good old hat. They'll probably bury me with it, but it's a good old hat. It's had a lot of wear, just getting it broke in good."*

Rusty Mauk. Just like his carvings, he's an original.

Rusty gets ready to feed the dog.

"What you do is take a log and cut off everything that doesn't look like an Indian."

Snapshot Biography

Rusty Mauk was born Nov. 22,1913, on the Cherokee Reservation in Oklahoma. He attended Augusta High School and married Hazel Cody March 24, 1934, in El Dorado. They have three children – Patricia Grisham, Rita Morgan and Rusty K. Mauk – three grandchildren and one great-granddaughter. Years in Kansas: 76.

An Old-Time Cowboy from the Old West

Jake McClure finds the telephone poles go by slower out near Cambridge

Cowboys. You don't see them much any more, at least not many like Jake McClure. Jake owns the Bar-O-Bar Ranch, which has been a family operation for generations. Jake keeps herds of 12 bison and 20 longhorn steers, partly to satisfy his need for the Old West and partly to entertain his family and friends and the people who pass by his ranch near Cambridge.

"I was raised up here in these hills, you know. And I've cowboyed all my life from start to finish. But I just love the wilder side. Of buffaloes and longhorns and all that."

His ranch seems to be a gathering place for people who also love the wilder side.

"People go down the road, the brake lights go on, they turn around and come back."

Jake, 71, is always happy to give them a tour or just let them admire his stock.

"I kinda look at the longhorn; they just seem to be part of our family around here. They can do just about anything they want to with their horns."

Jake particularly likes longhorns with a "Texas twist" — a little loop that throws itself into the horn before it spreads into a traditional longhorn shape. He likes it so much, in fact, that his waxed handlebar mustache shows a "Texas twist," too, before it curls up to accentuate his grin.

"Really, I don't know what I would do if I woke up some morning and the longhorns and buffaloes were gone. I'm sure I'd probably feel lost."

But he could find himself by harnessing a couple of horses to his wagon and going for a ride in the Flint Hills that he loves so. Or he could saddle up a couple of horses and go help his neighbors take care of their cattle, which he often does.

"The part I don't like is getting up early, but once I saddle up the horses . . . I forget all about having to get up. It's so pretty."

He rides with his 9-year-old daughter, Jessi Aldine, whom he and his wife adopted when the girl was 3 years old. She's lived with them since she was 6 months old, when Jake first sat her on the back of a horse and she held on.

"She's one heck of a rider. She rides as good as a lot of men."

He wants to give Jessi, and the people who come to his ranch, a taste of the West, whether it's looking at longhorns or hand-feeding one of the bison that have become spoiled by Jake's brand of care. He had to get rid of one buffalo because it simply was so tame it was dangerous. The animal would barrel toward Jake or anyone it thought might have feed.

"He'd just jump in the pickup with both feet and go to eating right out of the bucket."

Incidents like that, and the amount of work inherent in taking care of the animals, make some members of his family think it is time for him to take life a little easier.

"My brother and sister think that at my age it's time to get rid of all this nonsense. I'd miss them if I had to get rid of them."

Jake McClure and his daughter ride the Bar-O-Bar Ranch.

Jake did get rid of his four pair of oxen after driving them through the country and in countless parades. He donated some of his wagons and tack to area museums. He kept some of the carts and wagons, though, and still drives them with horses in parades in the area.

It's all part of the life and land Jake loves and isn't about to give up.

"It's just on the old-timey side where you go a little slower. You got more time to look at the telephone poles go by, and they don't go by as fast."

"It's just on the old-timey side where you go a little slower."

Snapshot Biography

Jake McClure was born Feb. 3, 1920, in Grand Summit. He attended eight years in a one-room schoolhouse and Grenola High School. He married Flora Aldine Harris on Valentine's Day, 1946, at her parents' ranch home east of Cambridge. They have three children: Ralph LeRoy II, Velma Aldine and Mary Alvina; an adopted daughter, Jessi Aldine; five grandchildren. Years in Kansas: 71.

The Perfect Way to Fry a Burger

Earl "Arkie" McGaugh's family has carried on tradition since 1917

Frying the perfect hamburger is an art the McGaugh family has been working at since 1917 when Earl's Cafe opened in a small Arkansas town. Earl McGaugh — who became known as "Arkie" immediately after moving to Kansas in 1951 — brought the family tradition to Wichita, where his Takhoma Burger has become a tradition of its own.

"My family's been frying hamburgers for 74 consecutive years, since 1917. I guess you could say practice makes perfect."

It's not just the toasted buns, the hand-cut fries or the bit of raw onion tucked inside each patty that brings in the customers to the tiny burger stand — it's Arkie himself.

In September 1990, Arkie came out of retirement to reopen the burger stand. He was so glad to be back at work that he composed a song for the occasion:

"He's back again, he's back again. Ol' Takhoma Arkie's in

again . . . . You'd think 40 years would change anything, but Arkie's burgers stay the same."

And Arkie hasn't forgotten that perfect way to fry a hamburger.

"I'll tell ya, a lot of people don't agree with me, but you have to have a thin patty, a hot griddle. You put it on a cold griddle, the flavor and juices get away. A hot griddle sears it.

"To toast the buns, you put the bottom on top. You squeeze it so the steam comes up through the bun, so there's no grease. It's no use teachin' most people how to do it.

"And a lot of people don't know how to sack. A lot of people want to do it with their right hand. It's a left-handed operation."

When Arkie first started flipping burgers as a boy in Arkansas, they were "a nickel, six for a quarter."

By 1990s' standards, Arkie's prices are still reasonable: a buck for a hamburger and $1.15 for a cheeseburger. When customers ask about seating, Arkie tells them to pick out any dry spot of grass out front they want.

Arkie keeps his business simple: burger, fries and a drink and no computer cash registers. He doesn't see any reason for such fancy gadgets.

"I thought about it a few times but then I remember my uncle back in Arkansas. His cash register consists of three chili bowls and a cigar box under the counter. And he done better than I did."

Arkie's dad opened Earl's Cafe in Waldron, Ark., in 1917 and later owned the Little Palace, which saw the family through the Depression.

"Seven boys and two girls were raised in that place."

After graduating from high school in 1940, Arkie worked for his dad until he joined the Army. In 1948 he opened his own McGaugh Cafe, which served plate lunches, breakfast and — of course — hamburgers. During the Korean War, people started moving out of Waldron and Arkie decided to try Kansas, where he heard the economy was better. He and his wife, Virgie, moved to Wichita in the fall of 1951 and on New Year's Day 1952 he fried his first hamburger at one of the

There's always a line at Takhoma Burger, but any customer will tell you it's well worth the wait.

city's four Takhoma Burgers.

In 1968 he bought the fixtures and the house next door to the remaining Takhoma Burger in a residential area west of downtown. He sold the business and tried to retire in 1980. For eight years someone else ran the burger stand and then it was closed because of the owner's health problems.

Arkie watched it sit vacant for six months, then donned his short-order cook's hat, which bears the Takhoma logo, and on Sept. 10, 1990, reopened the doors to his longtime customers — who have come from all 50 states. Takhoma Burger had become a family tradition for generations of Wichitans, and they welcomed him back — between mouthfuls.

And he's continuing to pass on the family tradition, this time to his grandson. It's a lot of work compared to retirement, but nothing like the 13 hours a day Arkie used to stand over a sizzling griddle.

"We're running it four hours a day. It ain't hurtin' either of us."

"My family's been frying hamburgers for 74 consecutive years, since 1917. I guess you could say practice makes perfect."

Snapshot Biography

Arkie was born Earl McGaugh on June 5, 1920, in Waldron, Ark. He graduated from Waldron High in 1940 and then went to work in his dad's cafe. He and his wife, Virgie, who were married in 1942, have two children, Lauren and Joyce, and five grandchildren. Years in Kansas: 40.

Applause in the Kansas Ozarks

Barry McGuire leaves the fast lane to settle in Elk Falls

Far from the lights of Broadway, a Kansas-born actor has found a niche for his love of theater and gardening in the tiny southeastern Kansas town of Elk Falls.

With any luck, Barry McGuire and a group of loyal local folks, who have banded together as the Friends of Elk Falls, hope to put the scenic town on the map by luring tourists to what they call the "Kansas Ozarks." In addition to the town's falls, they point proudly to a historic marker commemorating Prudence Crandall, a 19th century crusader against slavery, a unique pottery shop and — thanks to McGuire — a public garden and Sunday theater.

"This little ghost town . . . we've decided to put it on the map."

And now there are not just the Sunday visitors who drive their cars down Highway 160 into the tranquility of Elk Falls, but there's even an occasional bus tour stopping in town.

"I think some of us are calling it the village that time forgot. We are remote, yes, we are isolated, yes, but we have things that are rather intriguing to people who come through here."

When McGuire decided to "kind of retire" from show business in 1977, he set out to find a place to live. With roots firmly in the Midwest — his grandfather had homesteaded on the Cherokee Strip in 1893 — his thoughts returned to his home state, where he hadn't lived since leaving for college in 1948.

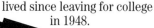

"I kept having this pull to come back to Kansas for whatever reason. I kept being drawn back to Kansas."

He chose Elk Falls, 65 miles east of Arkansas City, where he had graduated from high school. After a few years there he was lured back to the theater by the Indiana Repertory Theatre, where he stayed for five seasons. But again he decided to return to Kansas and Elk Falls, and this time he bought some badly overgrown vacant lots and started putting in flower beds, creating what would soon become the Elk Falls Garden.

"Now we've had over 2,000 visitors from 19 states and six foreign countries.

"The garden has presented me with a wonderful opportunity to be in show business again because it is a display garden and people come here and when I see their enjoyment and their oohs and ahhs, it's kind of like walking out and taking a bow."

But as of summer 1991, McGuire can actually take a bow after performances in a church hall he bought and turned into a theater. For his weekly performances in the Elk Falls Village Variety Theatre, he calls on not only his acting experience, but his talents as a puppeteer and magician.

"Every Sunday afternoon I get back on the boards."

In 1952, armed with a degree in theater and a one-way bus ticket to the Big Apple — bought with $50 given to him by the playwright of a summer show he'd acted in — McGuire set out to find fame and fortune. Within two weeks he'd been cast in a professional children's theater production.

Not yet realizing the ways of Broadway, he then brazenly called up the producers of a Broadway play and asked for an audition — which he landed, even without an agent. He was cast as understudy to the lead and though he never got on stage McGuire considered it his "big break" because he got his equity card and the experience opened doors to other shows, summer stock and live television shows. One of his most memorable roles was playing opposite Debbie Reynolds in a Chicago stage production of "The Actress."

By the end of the 1950s, however, the television

industry had up and moved to Hollywood and McGuire decided to follow it.

"I held out as long as I could. I never should have moved. It was a big mistake. I didn't care for working in film.

"I was trained for the stage. If you were on Broadway you had to be good, but in California that wasn't the case. They prided themselves on finding a girl in a drugstore and making her a star."

However, he landed roles in several television shows, including "Gunsmoke," "Father Knows Best" and "The Real McCoys." In 1964 he decided to try something else and he worked for the parks and recreation department for a while, before concentrating on being a free-lance magician and puppeteer, which included appearances at the Magic Castle.

In the 1970s he took over the puppet theater at Santa's Village in California, but then he decided to leave the show business world of California behind for good and he found himself in Elk Falls.

"One could buy a house here for next to nothing and it was quiet and peaceful and remote. At that particular point in my life it was something I was looking for."

He opened the gardens to the public in 1986 and in 1991 opened the Elk Falls Village Variety Theatre.

"We're getting a good little crowd, considering there's no advertising and we're out in the middle of nowhere."

But most of the time McGuire doesn't mind the isolation. There's his cat Groucho and he has many friends among the town's 100 residents. Buying a loaf of bread, however, is a 12-mile round-trip jaunt to either Moline or Longton, and more serious grocery shopping must be done in Winfield or Independence. Prior to opening the theater, McGuire spent the long Kansas winters reading. Now, however, he's planning on spending them preparing for the next season, which runs from May through October.

"I like being alone very much. I find I'm pretty good company."

He admits he'd give it all up if the right part came along, but for now he's content to play his current role in Elk Falls. And, yes, he admits Kansas does have its drawbacks.

"It's hot, the chiggers eat me alive, but I feel at home here. You can take the boy out of Kansas but . . . here I am."

McGuire with puppet co-stars.

Snapshot Biography

Barry McGuire was born in Caldwell on March 7, 1930. He attended the University of Washington-Seattle and the University of Denver, where he earned a bachelor of arts degree in theater in 1952. Years in Kansas: 33.

Barry McGuire with a photo from "The Actress" in which he starred opposite Debbie Reynolds.

Straightening Rims and People's Lives

Charles Moore of Wichita charges for one service; the other is free

Old buildings downtown. Buildings that smell of hot metal, twisted iron and a man's sweat. Charles Moore will straighten your wheels or he'll straighten your life. The wheels and rims are Charles's pulpit.

"All these wheels I got, over there and over there, they're straight. You can take 'em and put them right on your car."

Working in a hard-to-find and almost forgotten building near downtown Wichita, Charles says bent wheels are a lot like people's lives. Some are off-center, some wobble a bit. Charles makes them straight.

His business is Charles Moore Rim Straightening, located just a few blocks from downtown Wichita. He doesn't do much advertising.

"It's mainly word of mouth from the work I do."

But the word of God is important, too. Charles is an associate pastor at St. Andrew's Missionary Baptist Church. He not only speaks from the pulpit on the word of God, but sometimes the word comes out while he's hammering on rims.

"Some customers bring up the spiritual, and sometimes I can get a spiritual question or point in."

Even at the age of 68, Charles still works five days a week, and his son, Byron, helps out. This is definitely a labor-intensive business, but there's an art to it too, he says.

"Now see, that wheel is perfect. That'll run straight on your car."

For much of his life, he has been trying to shape metal and people's lives. Moore has lived in Wichita since 1952, and worked as a welder and for an axle

and wheel alignment service before starting his wheel rim-straightening business.

He charges $12 to straighten a regular wheel, but his advice on life is free. Both services, Charles says, are likely to stay at the same price. His pastoring is something he does because of his faith.

Folks are sometimes surprised to find a minister among oil and metal and noise.

"I tell all of them at church and Sunday school, we got to do the best we can . . . ."

Fate steered Charles toward starting his own business. In November 1980, while working for a wheel alignment service, a tire blew up. Both of Charles' arms required surgery. After recuperating, he decided to start his own business.

So if you stop by to see Charles Moore, you'll hear about a marriage that has lasted 48 years, a son who died in his teens, and a work accident that helped him start his own business. Most of all, you'll meet a simple and charming man.

"All these wheels I got, over there and over there, they're straight. You can take 'em and put them right on your car."

Snapshot Biography

Charles Moore was born on Oct. 7, 1923, in Texas. His family moved to Lenapah, Okla., in the early 1930s. He served in the military in World War II, then returned to Oklahoma. Moore moved to Wichita in 1952 and worked as a welder and later for an axle and wheel alignment service. He started his business, Charles Moore Rim Straightening, in November 1983. He is an associate minister at St. Andrew's Missionary Baptist Church. He and his wife Nola were married in 1943. They had two daughters and four sons, one of whom died in 1972. They also have nine grandchildren and two great-grandchildren. Years in Kansas: 39.

Turning Barn-Wood into Art
Ike Neufeld of Arlington creates three-dimensional pictures

After Ike Neufeld retired from the trucking business 12 years ago, he and his wife, Mildred, moved to a small acreage in the country near Arlington. There, the tulips bloom and the windmill turns — and barn-wood turns into art.

Neufeld slices and saws lumber from old, weathered barns and pieces it into intricate rustic scenes.

"I use wood that's at least a hundred years old."

Neufeld tore down a barn on his property to get his century-old cottonwood and cedar and pine woods.

"It's seen a lot of weather — sunshine and rain, snow, hail, what have you. There's no way of making that wood, except let Mother Nature do it. That's the only way it can happen."

And it does happen, with a lot of help from Ike.

"I don't know how I got started. It just happened. I made one and came in and showed my wife and she said, "I think you've got something."

She still has it.

All of his barn-wood pictures are three-dimensional and are all original.

"It takes a lot of time, for sure. Time, patience and imagination. I don't make anything absolutely square straight; that way you can't say it's a kit . . . . I get something started, and then I keep working to see what comes out of it. If I get a picture made out of it, and hang it up in somebody's house, it might get to be another hundred years old. I just like to get the picture done so I can see what I've done . . . . It takes a lot of patience and imagination, but I've still got all my fingers."

Ike tosses the pictures he doesn't like into a wood-burning stove nearby. His finished products, though, have never been rejected. Not counting the pictures he has given away for birthdays, anniversaries and Christmases, all 730-some pieces have been purchased by buyers from across the country and in Canada.

"If somebody wants something for someone who has everything, they come to me . . . . I'm very well pleased that I can do something that other people can enjoy. If you can do something that gives other people pleasure, I think you're making your mark."

Ike likes creating barn-wood art because it keeps him busy. Sometimes, though, the workshop closes in and he escapes with Mildred for a little relaxation.

"You got to get away from it and do something else like we do — go out and play golf. This is a meadow-muffin golf course. Five holes out in the pasture . . . . We did have flags up there, but they'd wear out. Cattle pull them off, so I just put plastic jugs up."

Snapshot Biography

Ike Neufeld was born Oct. 23, 1912, in Henderson Neb. He attended Thomas Grove School in Reno County. He married Mildred Gitchel on Dec. 24, 1937, in Hutchinson. They have four children–James John, Nancy Jean, Eva Nell and Kenneth Ray– seven grandchildren and three great-grandchildren. Years in Kansas: 76.

A Hardware Store with 100,000 Items

Kelly Nichols owns the entire business district in Harlan

About a thousand curious visitors from across the country each year find their way down Highway 281 into Harlan, population 19, in north-central Smith County. They come looking for the town's general store, the last surviving business in this once-thriving town.

They're not disappointed by its proprietor, Kelly Nichols, who opened the hardware store in 1928. While the out-of-towners come to marvel at the 100,000 items he has piled outside and inside his store, the locals come for groceries, hardware items, candy, cigars, and the Wolverine boots and shoes he carries.

"I sell one to five pairs a week. They come from as far away as up into Nebraska. They don't have a Wolverine store closer than Phillipsburg."

Kelly has collected items for more than half a century, and much of it crowds the store's aisles. There are potatoes from his garden, razorblades (10 for 10 cents), crutches, fan belts, lamps, hoses, rakes, plows, tools, baling wire — and, on occasion, even pheasant.

"Oh yes, I sell lots of them. Last year, I skinned 45 the first Saturday night of season."

In his 63 years in business, Kelly has found that eventually someone will want what he has kept.

"I told my wife it didn't make any difference what you kept, if you kept it long enough, someday somebody'll come by that wants it."

But can he find everything amid the tens of thousands of items that crowd the store?

"If it hasn't been too long since I put it there."

Kelly, who lives in quarters built on behind the store, claims to be retired, but the store is still open every single day. He has slowed down on adding to his inventory, however.

"I don't buy too much stuff anymore. Though a lady brought in 30 small lamps the other day and I bought them."

He had a fire wagon in Harlan for quite a while, and though it's now gone, he helps out as a volunteer fireman at such activities as the firemen's lunch stand at the Labor Day festivities in Gaylord, "the next town west."

While there's still a church in town, Kelly fears it too will disappear from Harlan. On a recent Sunday, the United Methodist Church drew only six worshippers. Once, the church and Nichols Hardware were among many bustling businesses, including a lumberyard, in the railroad town. Harlan even boasted a college between 1888 and 1889, and the dormitory still stands near the town's deserted Main Street.

Kelly figures the town's businesses starting dying out in the 1930s. Now, he's the only one left.

He greets locals, who drop by for bottles of pop or to buy a few items they can't get elsewhere. Many do their shopping in Osborne or Smith Center. He keeps a book in which he asks out-of-town visitors to register. Some have come from as far away as China and Alaska to see the old-time hardware store.

"I had 1,019 last year. I give 'em a pen with my name and advertising on it."

All of Kelly Nichols' garages are filled to the brim.

> *"I told my wife it didn't make any difference what you kept, if you kept it long enough, someday somebody'll come by that wants it."*

The gas pump may be out of service, but anything else you happen to want you can find at Kelly Nichols' place.

Snapshot Biography

Kelly Nichols was born Sept. 7, 1905, two miles south of his current store in Harlan. He married Jessie Doll in 1924 in nearby Smith Center. In 1991, Kelly lost his wife, who died March 31, and his daughter Eileen and son-in-law, who were killed in a car accident. He has one grandson who lives nearby and two great-granddaughters. When he graduated from Harlan High School in 1925, there were 60 students in the high school. It closed in the 1950s. Years in Kansas: 86.

Doll Doctor Repairs Broken Memories
Evelyn Padget of Dodge City brings her patients back to life

Evelyn with one of many patients.

Playing with dolls can be a key part of childhood memories, and there's a woman in Dodge City who understands that. She's made a business of repairing some of those memories.

They arrive broken and battered. Evelyn Padget makes them well. Evelyn is Dodge City's "doll doctor." The dolls are her patients.

"Some of them come in and you think, 'They had a hectic life somewhere along the line.' The nice thing about it is they don't lie there and cry or anything. They just wait for you to put them back together."

After years of neglect, it can take up to six months to repair a doll.

"Well, see, you've got to get all this old paint off. This is another reason why you can't have fingernails. It takes a lot of time and effort. Then you fill that in with wood filler. Then it has to be sanded and sanded. Then I put on more filler. . . and a sealer. Then I sand some more, put on more filler, more sealer. You put on as high as three to four coats. I paint features on with enamel because that's what they usually have used."

Evelyn hung out her shingle as a doll doctor in 1977, after a little pushing from her friends. She really did not need a second job to keep her busy. Evelyn already was office manager for a Dodge City construction firm, from which she retired in 1988 after 30 years. But she had completed a correspondence course in dressmaking and, later, one in doll repair from the Lifetime Career School in Los Angeles. Friends began bringing her dolls to fix and, since then, her bedside manner has pulled many a doll from destruction.

"They act like they're glad you're working on them and trying to fix them up. Now that sounds like I'm senile, it really does — when you start talking to dolls, but they don't talk back."

But to Evelyn, the dolls take on personalities as she sands and sculpts and paints them back to life.

"Each one is kind of a challenge to see what you're going to make out of it. I don't know; it seems it's just fun. It's just like anybody else's hobby, I do believe. They enjoy it or they wouldn't do it at all."

Her doll business has other benefits, too.

"It's the people that you meet and the stories you hear about the dolls that really intrigue you. You hear some of the nicest stories and some sad stories. . . I get my pleasure out of doing something for someone that gives them pleasure. Really, that's all you get out of life, is what you do for somebody else."

Most of her patients are heirlooms, not dolls the dealers will resell. As a result, she often cannot buy wigs and arms and legs or other replacement parts. The companies that manufacture collectors' dolls do not want them repaired or restored later. That forces Evelyn to haunt auctions and garage sales, looking for abandoned dolls much like auto-body repairmen search through salvage yards for parts.

"And I bought out two doll hospitals, which was wrong. I need a barn. I took the garage over and made it into my shop. You can get around in there, if you're careful."

Evelyn has one special doll in her shop that you might not expect to see. That doll is in the form of a Tom Selleck poster plastered on Evelyn's back door.

"Isn't he darling? I think he is just a handsome man. I really like watching him. You men like to watch girls, so I don't know why us girls can't have some of the men."

Evelyn Padget. One of Kansas' real-life dolls.

"They act like they're glad you're working on them and trying to fix them up."

112

Evelyn in her garage workshop

Snapshot Biography

Evelyn Padget was born Dec. 22, 1921, in Dodge City. She attended Dodge City High School and Dodge City Community College. She married Clifford Padget March 7, 1947, in Dodge City. They have two children, Clifton Padget and Glenda Shaw; two grandchildren and two great-grandchildren. Years in Kansas: 70.

Note-Takers on the Byways of Kansas

Mil and Marci Penner of Inman travel back roads to tell a state's story

For many of us, it would be a parent's dream. A daughter returns home to work with her dad. For Mil Penner, it's a dream come true. Mil and his daughter Marci are a father-daughter team whose books you might have in your library.

They've just finished their second joint book project, *Kansas Event Guide*. Their first, published in 1990, was *Kansas Weekend Guide*.

For Marci, the book projects with her dad have become a labor of love and fun.

"We'll get in the van and travel for hours, days really, and we'll just talk and talk and talk," she said.

Both books were born out of a family's love for the land and its people.

Marci returned to Kansas in 1990 after spending nearly five years in Philadelphia as an elementary school counselor. But an illness accelerated a growing feeling that she needed to return home.

"Coming back here . . . the subtle beauty of this state and the subtle beauty of relationships and family . . . .

"I'm tired of this going home at Christmas and a week in the summer, talking to them just on the phone. I want to be back with Mom and Dad and the farm and my relatives."

It was on the farm near Inman where Marci was born. Mil has lived all his life in the Inman area. Of German stock, his schooling was more challenging than most. He was raised by parents who spoke only "low German," and that is all he knew.

"The first day of school was a heck of a big

surprise. I couldn't talk to a soul."

Now, the words of the English language are the tools for both his vocation and avocation. But it wasn't always that way. Mil was a farmer, then got into the earth-moving and irrigation business. A growing concern for the environment, however, prompted him to make a 180-degree turn. Today, conservation and the preservation of Kansas wildlife and its land are high priorities, and those themes are reflected in his writing.

Mil's first venture into writing was with fellow Kansan Carol Schmidt, and they produced two books: *Kansas Journeys* and *Prairie: The Land and Its People*. For him, producing these books were emotional experiences.

"But the first thought that flashes through my mind is my one little granddaughter . . . and I see geese flying in the sky and I want her to see it someday, and to experience the joy. I want her to feel what Marci's feeling now, and I would like to be able to preserve this for her."

When the first book from the Penner team came out, Marci got excited.

"The book itself means a lot, but to have done it with your dad is. . . . We had a ball. The first time I held the book in my hands and I saw Mil and Marci Penner, boy, that was a rush . . . that was something else."

The Penners traveled throughout the state, with pen and camera, taking pictures of places and things many of us might pass by.

"My wish would be that everyone would go to those places that we went and enjoy it as much as we did," Marci said.

Even the folks back in Philadelphia get a chance to enjoy what Marci does through regular writings she sends them. She titles these writings "Prairie Tales":

"Have you ever actually really seen a robin extract a worm from the earth? I did today. Quick as a flash, that robin pounced on the sub-terranean creature and it was gone. . . .

"Mom and Dad are successfully luring a wild turkey hen and a nice duck couple to the farm . . . .

"The Inman Ledger reported the only thing left of the old Curt's Electric Store is the

Dave Balzer talks with Mil and Marci Penner near the Stan Herd mural in Inman. Balzer helped organize the effort to have the mural done.

thermometer that has a two digit phone number on it."

Marci describes their *modus operandi* this way: Besides talking up a storm, their work on the book involves Mil doing the photography.

"When we get to a town, I go one way and he goes the other and we interview separately," Marci said. *"We've made many friends across the state. . . .I keep thinking I'm not working 'cause it's too much fun."*

While the weekend guide book is a collection of special places across the state, most on the back roads of life, the event guide highlights community festivals and events throughout the year in Kansas. In fact, the Penners now sponsor their own event in October, The Kansas Sampler Festival.

At this year's event in October, there were more than 100 exhibitors of arts and crafts. There's even a parade. An estimated 5,000 people attended the festivities.

Of course, Mil and Marci sold a few books that weekend, too, but you get the feeling if they can just break even on each new book venture, that's all the motivation they need to head down the road for their next adventure to tell more of the Kansas story.

"We're touching the heart, the spirit of Kansas, I think," Mil said.

Mil and Marci Penner study a road map as they plan the route for their next journey along Kansas highways and byways.

Snapshot Biography

Mil Penner was born on Jan. 16, 1929, near Inman and spoke only "low German" until entering grade school. He graduated from Inman High School and attended Bethel College in Newton. He then began farming, and later became involved in the earthmoving and irrigation business. Mil changed careers in 1985 when he began writing. He married V. Lee in 1950 and they have two daughters, Marci of Inman, and Liz King of Boulder; a son, Murray, who lives near Wichita; and one grandchild. Years in Kansas: 62.

Snapshot Biography

Marci Penner was born on Feb. 2, 1956, on the Penner farm near Inman. She graduated from high school in 1974. Marci attended the University of Kansas, where she was an athlete and received a bachelors degree in 1979, majoring in radio, television and film. In 1985, she received a masters in counseling and guidance from the University of Wisconsin. She was an elementary counselor in the Philadelphia area for five years, then returned to Inman in 1990. Years in Kansas: 25.

The Voice of Hutchinson

'Perky' retires after making many radio friends

After 34 years on the air, Wilma "Perky" Perks retired June 14, 1991, as host of the popular Hutchinson radio show, "Party Line."

"Of course I miss the work. Being on the radio was fun. And I miss the people but now when I go downtown, several people will recognize me and stop to chat."

Every weekday for three and a half decades, Perky presided over the community exchange. She took calls from people who had something to sell, who needed a job or wanted to talk. She gave news items, such as birth announcements. But most of all she enjoyed what she calls her mission work, beating the drum for community organizations, telling of their needs and their fund drives. Listeners loved it and tuned in every weekday morning from 9:45 to 11 to hear her and follow her urging to become involved in bettering the community.

In 1983, when she found she had cancer and had to have a mastectomy and a hysterectomy, in typical Perky fashion she told her listeners all about it. She urged them to watch for cancer signals and to overcome fears that sometimes keep people from seeking timely treatment. While taking chemotherapy she even had her physician give her a treatment during the program, to show that cancer patients often can carry on normal lives.

"I was on chemotherapy for 52 weeks and I didn't miss a day at the microphone. Now I take all the tests for active cells. I get a pap smear and breast exam regularly. Nothing has recurred."

Perky joined KWBW at the age of 23 as a secretary who found herself keeping the station's logs of shows and commercials, writing commercials and anything else that came to hand.

"There was another Wilma at the station then. One of the kids in the church choir called me Perky and I suggested that they call me that, to avoid confusion."

In those early days the station ran community service announcements – for meetings, fund drives and the like – in with the news. But the free announcements began to overwhelm the news, and station manager Fred L. Conger suggested an on-air Bulletin Board, with Perky making the announcements. It worked so well that shortly he decided to expand her scope and created Party Line. Soon everyone within range of the station knew Perky and her clear, fast-paced voice that exudes a caring as well as a let's-get-the-job-done tone.

"My voice is different. They would recognize me when I was out somewhere. I had never done on-air work. I guess people liked the program because it was folksy."

Besides making a host of friends for her, the program brought her more awards than she can count.

"The Civitans gave me their Citizen of the Year award; they don't give out many of those. The Salvation Army gave me its Ken Kest Award for outstanding volunteer service. When Mike Hayden was governor, he gave me an award for being outstanding volunteer in the state."

She abandoned the microphone because she turned 62 and her husband, Dean F. Perks, had been retired for several years. She wanted to spend more time with him and do some traveling. One of their projects was to move a mobile home to Cottonwood Lake, west of Sterling. They planned to spend a couple of idyllic days a week there.

"Then on August 30 a storm dropped out of the sky and did a lot of damage. Our trailer ended up in 20 feet of water and we've been spending our time tracking down information for insurance. It's unbelievable, what you have to have."

Insurance troubles in the past, Perky is racing through her busy fall schedule. She organized and directed the annual Perky's Garage Sale, which takes place in a rented fairgrounds building each November. This year she is in charge of the Salvation Army's Christmas programs in Hutchinson: distribution of food, bell-ringing, wrapping and distributing gifts – in a word – everything.

She also serves on committees and executive boards of the Salvation Army and its Soup Kitchen, Friendship Meals, Girl Scouts, Retired Senior Volunteer Program and the American Cancer Society. Perky also teaches two Bible classes in low-income housing units for those over age 60. Somehow she finds time to do the handwork she loves and to use the knitting machine the station gave her as a parting gift. Moreover, she keeps her hand in broadcasting by doing occasional remotes from businesses and the mall.

Perky and Bob Watson, KWBW control board operator, go over plans for the morning "Party Line" show.

Wilma Perks in an on-air interview.

Snapshot Biography

Wilma Perks was born May 28, 1929, in Hutchinson. She graduated from Hutchinson High School and a private secretarial school. She was secretary for the county superintendent of schools before moving to KWBW. She married Dean F. Perks in 1947. Years in Kansas: 62.

Hunters of Garage Sale Treasures

Sue and B.J. Pierce of Mulvane don't believe in the word 'new'

Owning things second-hand has become second nature for Sue and B.J. Pierce, whose old-fashioned Mulvane home is packed from top to bottom with items bought at hundreds of auctions and garage sales. There is nothing store-bought in their creatively decorated home.

"People just don't realize they can furnish their house with little to nothing," Sue says. "We wish we would have gotten into it earlier because we lived without a lot of things, because we thought you had to spend a lot of money."

Attending garage sales — sometimes as many as 70 or 80 in one weekend — has been a weekend custom since the early days of their marriage in 1976 in Emporia.

"We were gone every weekend," says B.J., who would often come home from auctions with a truckload of goods. "I would go to auctions every weekend, come home with a couple hundred dollars worth of stuff, and rearrange the house every weekend."

Even their clothes, from swimsuits to shoes to underwear, are bought at a fraction of their original retail price.

When they were first married, they'd get up as early as 4 a.m. to hit the garage sales in Emporia, where the deals are better than in the Wichita area.

The Pierces in a bedroom "decorated" from their weekend sojourns to auctions and garage sales. Their children, Jonathan and Hannah, often accompany them.

They've perfected a shopping routine that includes Sue carrying the diaper wipes and B.J. getting down on his hands and knees to rummage through boxes under the tables.

"That's where the treasures are," Sue says.

But some of it is more than luck, Sue thinks.

"People we talk to at garage sales think it's being in the right place at the right time. But I think it's our heavenly Father, I really do."

Though many items are bought for a nickel or dime, their prize purchase was a dining room set.

"This solid walnut table, buffet, six chairs, we paid $200 for the whole outfit," B.J. recalls. "If you went to an antique store, most likely you couldn't touch the buffet itself for $200."

Though there is little room left in their 2,400-square-foot home and attic for more items, the only thing that's slowed them down is the adoption of two children — Hannah and Jonathan — who don't mind the hand-me-downs. However, Sue finds she can no longer spend all day Saturday on the road. Now she has to be back in time for lunch, or if they take a lunch with them, they have to be back home by nap time. But the sales have certainly helped clothe and take care of two children.

"The baby bed was $30," Sue recalls. "The stuffed animals in it . . . 5, 10,15 cents here and there."

The Pierces aren't afraid to raise their children in a home filled with fragile knickknacks.

"We don't want to raise them in a sterile environment," Sue says. "We did put the kerosene lamps up a little higher."

They like not only the price but the quality of older items.

"There's just so many things that you can get at a cheap price that you couldn't get at a store," B.J. says. "Many times you find things you couldn't buy at a store."

And there have been times when the tables have turned and the Pierces have had their own garage sale. In fact, one three-day sale netted them $3,500 — and they only sold things that were not their "favorites." Another sale they billed as the End of the

Trail Sale and advertised with signs in the shape of a covered wagon.

They've learned that what is trash now could indeed be a treasure in years to come. Sue, who collects old tins, realizes that current containers may someday be collectibles, so she saves everything.

"Our home is really, really original," Sue says of their eclectic surroundings.

But it's highly organized — the wooden crates and 20-some trunks are filled to capacity with quilts, magazines, paper sacks, blankets, rugs. No space is wasted — and it's all dusted every other week. The cleaning regimen is a full-day project. Even her Christmas, birthday and anniversary shopping is done at garage sales.

"My sister's a junkie, too. We made a deal; for Christmas we just trade junk."

B.J. and Susan's 15 year cache includes children Jonathan and Hannah.

Snapshot Biography

B.J. Pierce was born in Brookhaven, Miss., Oct. 24, 1951. Sue was born in Wichita, June 15, 1953. She graduated from Washington High School in Kansas City and he graduated from Abilene High School and later attended Hutchinson Junior College and Emporia State University. They were married Feb. 17, 1976, and started attending garage sales soon after. They have two adopted children, Hannah and Jonathan. Years in Kansas: B.J., 37; Sue, 38.

A Real Champion of a Fiddler

Perseverance pays off for Jeff Pritchard of Valley Center

Jeff Pritchard is a national award-winning bluegrass fiddle player. Through his fingers comes music from the heart.

"Music is just one way to express myself. It's one way I can show what I can do . . . I guess sometimes what I can't do also."

A decade ago Jeff thought his career was finished. As he was building a home for his parents near Valley Center, an accident with a circular saw almost ended his music. It severed one finger and cut two others in half.

"When I had to stop fiddling, it was like taking away food from a guy who's eating. Fiddling is a release for me. It's how I relax and have fun."

Jeff, who is 34, has been fiddling since junior high school days. He had been playing the violin since he was in the third grade and was getting a little tired of it.

"Then I went to an old-time fiddlers contest. Those people were smiling. Classical musicians don't smile. They are so serious. I couldn't get over the way those fiddlers were having fun."

So he took up fiddling, and he too had fun and won all sorts of awards. Then came the day in 1979 when the accident occurred. Doctors reimplanted the middle finger and repaired the others. But the bones did not mend properly. He got a staph infection. The prognosis for his hand was grim and he feared he would never fiddle again.

"But I decided to look for the very best and we found Hand Surgery Associates in Louisville, Kentucky, who do nothing but work on hands. They fixed me up. And they broke the tip of my middle finger and bent it so I could play the fiddle. There is no flexion in the outer joints. It worked. Two months later I was playing. The night of my birthday Mom and I tried to play for the first time. I was flabbergasted. I couldn't believe it could come back as easy as it did."

He again got into competitive fiddling, traveling around the country to different festivals and often winning awards. Then in 1986 he won the Grand Masters Award in Nashville. Part of the award is the opportunity to play at the Grand Ole Opry and he did that in 1987, then served as a judge for the Grand Masters. Having reached the top, he quit competition.

"It takes so much time to be competitive. I used to practice three or four hours a day. By the time you take expenses off your winnings, nobody is making a living at it. You almost have to be living at home or be in college. In terms of who's winning big in fiddling contests, I am an old man."

But Jeff didn't give up the fiddle. Until early in 1991 he played with the Wichita Linemen band. Then he became fiddle-guitarist for the four-man Kaw-Cajuns, which includes a guitarist, bass guitarist and drummer. They play for barn parties, weddings and other occasions, sometimes three or four times a week.

"Fiddling has opened up many doors for me. My partner, Graham Dorian, also is a fiddler. He and I formed TFI — that's Twin Fiddlers Inc. — and bought Hidden Lakes, a golf course and country club in Wichita, in May (1991)."

Jeff's business-finance major at Wichita State University comes in handy as does the fact that he's been a pilot, flying a Cessna 185, for eight years. His life is filled with business, his young family and with fiddling.

"I married Kim Suzanne on September 17, 1988. I met her because she was selling advertising on KFDI and worked for a client of mine. I liked her, and then I found out she rides horseback and likes country music. On August 10, 1991, our baby was born. We had a couple of names picked out. One of them was Jake Tanner. In the hospital, someone said that sounds like a fiddler. That did it! We named him Jake Tanner Pritchard."*

Jeff's parents, Paul and Mary, live in Valley Center. Mary, who played violin in high school and college, encouraged her son to take up the instrument. When he turned to fiddling, she followed suit. Now she collects fiddles and plays with the Kansas Ramblers.

Looking back on his early days playing the violin, Jeff makes this comparison:

"There's a lot of difference between the violin and the fiddle. You carry your violin in a case but you carry a fiddle in a gunny sack. Violinists play music the same way each time. Fiddlers take the basic melody and improvise on it. They never play the same way twice. Old-time fiddling was a real American art, handed down from father to son. That's why we once had distinct regional styles, but that's going by the wayside now. Fiddling is even more homogenized now than it was 15 years ago, but we have some really good players today."

Mary Pritchard plays the accordion while son Jeff fiddles.

"You carry your violin in a case but you carry a fiddle in a gunny sack."

Snapshot Biography

Jeff Pritchard was born Nov. 17, 1957, in Wichita. He graduated from Wichita North High and earned a business-finance degree at WSU in 1979. He married Kim Suzanne Sellers Sept. 17, 1988, and they have one son. Years in Kansas: 34.

Capturing Old West in Bronze
Frank Reese Sr. of Lindsborg gives new life to western scenes

The bronze sculptures stand in the Hitching Post Studio, a tribute to the Old West captured by an artist some might call a maverick. A heart attack made Frank Reese Sr. — who grew up thinking artists were sissies — turn seriously to the craft in 1972. The Lindsborg self-taught artist, now 69, is more at home in overalls and on a horse than with the world of art, where his sculptures bring several thousand dollars each.

His sculptures are in private collections across the country, including that of former President Reagan. Frank sent one of his bighorn sheep sculptures to Reagan in 1983 after learning that the president had such sheep on his ranch.

Frank's sculptures capture the essence of the Old West, from the tiny details on a cavalry horse's saddle to Indian artifacts. He has put people from his own life into his sculptures and the animals are meticulously crafted by Reese, who grew up working cattle and horses on his grandfather's farm near Abilene. For a new sculpture that depicts a scene from the Civil War era, Frank studied books of saddles from the period and uncovered a real buffalo skeleton to use as a model.

"You gotta get everything right. Ninety-nine won't know the difference, but one will and he can't wait to tell ya."

To Frank, sculpting is no special talent. He wonders why everyone can't reproduce what they see.

"To me, I think everybody should be able to copy anything they see. If you can see it, I don't know why you can't reproduce it."

The natural talent seems to run in the family and Frank said that three of his four children "could be artists if they wanted." Daughter Susan is an artist in Santa Fe, N.M., and his dad did hand engravings.

"Susan could draw pictures before she could go to school, soon as she got a pencil in her hand."

A high school dropout, Frank never had an art lesson.

"You can't read books. It won't do you any good to go to school if you don't have some idea of what an animal looks like. . . . The best way to learn is to make a mistake."

His father was a boxer and a farmer, and the last thing Frank thought he'd be is an artist. But a heart attack forced him to change his lifestyle at the age of 50. Prior to that, Frank had made a steel sculpture by pounding and welding, and he began to explore the wax sculpturing and bronze casting, which proved much easier and allowed for greater detail. He even created his own foundry to cast the sculptures, but now they are sent to a foundry in Oklahoma for the expensive and time-consuming process. In 1984, he built the Hitching Post Studio adjacent to his house, on a quiet dirt road just off the highway in Lindsborg.

Frank doesn't think he'll ever run out of subjects.

"I got more ideas than I got money."

It can cost thousands of dollars to have a single sculpture cast in bronze so it isn't feasible for Frank to have many sitting in galleries, though he has sold a number that way, in Lindsborg and in Kansas City.

"A lot of galleries want 'em, but they want me to put up the money so I just keep 'em at home. They're better off sitting here, selling one now and then."

His home studio is visited often by tourists to Lindsborg or groups of school children. In summer 1991, he was working on his 32nd sculpture; each one is cast between 20 and 50 times. Prices for a single animal start at $400.

After attending high school in Gypsum, Frank decided to go to trade school, attracted by the high wages — $2.25 an hour — Boeing was paying at the time. Frank was then making $1 a day working on the farm. He finished the course and at the age of 18 became a machinist at Boeing in 1941, where he worked until 1944 when he joined the military. After serving for two years, he began farming and farmed until 1961, finally quitting because "I didn't like the government telling me what to do." He then bought a welding business and moved to Lindsborg.

Some of his sculptures are of a single animal — a buffalo or horse, for instance — and others are scenes that tell a story, such as the one where a cowboy is flung from his horse by a charging buffalo, which actually happened to Frank. Or there's his favorite sculpture, "The Gift of the Great Spirit," in which an Indian makes an offering to the gods before a hunt.

Frank's patience is endless: He spent seven months trying to perfect a horse's mane so it would be as flowing in bronze as it is in real life. But don't ask his secret; he won't tell. And some pieces, such as Indian feathers, are poured in bronze separately and then attached to enrich their realism.

The result is pioneer women, Indians, cowboys, buffalo and other vestiges of the Old West crafted in lines so graceful they seem to contradict the hard-edged bronze that has captured them for eternity.

To Frank, sculpting is no special talent. He wonders why everyone can't reproduce what they see.

Reese uses real buffalo bones and consults vintage photos to enhance the authenticity of his work.

Snapshot Biography

Frank Reese Sr. was born Oct. 9, 1922, in Gypsum. He married Laura in 1943. They have four children – John Reese, Pat Stewart, Frank Robert "Bob," Susan Reese McCawley, five grandchildren and two great-grandchildren. Years in Kansas: 69.

Frank Reese applies the finishing touch.

Mrs. Kansas Keeps Priorities Straight

Lou Ann Ritchie of Wichita balances cover-girl career with family life

The face of a certain Wichita woman may look familiar, although you may not remember where you saw her. It could have been on a billboard, in a magazine or on television.

Lou Ann Ritchie, a Newton native, has been associated with international modeling for years, with the Ford Modeling Agency in New York and the Tanya Blair Agency in Dallas. She has modeled for Vogue, Oscar de la Renta, General Motors, Mary Kay Cosmetics, Neiman Marcus, Dillard's and Crest toothpaste, and was the exclusive national billboard model for Canadian Club.

"It's hard work. It's like any other job. It's something I enjoy, though; I love it a lot. I get to wear beautiful clothes — I love clothes and I love marketing — but it's tough, like any job is."

The job can take her away for days at a time from her husband, Jack, and their sons, Sammy and Cole.

"The minute you're away from them, the minute they go to school, I wonder what they're doing and you always want to be there for everything. But it's good for me, because it makes me appreciate them even more. I'm so glad to be home . . . it makes me so thankful for them and for what I do have here in Wichita. I've established my priorities and I know what's most important in my life, and that's my family."

She credits her husband for being the "motivator" in her modeling career. She had done local fashion

shows and commercials and, about six months after the birth of Sammy, Jack suggested they go to Dallas to try to affiliate with an agency for national work.

"He was just there with me every step of the way. It's the kind of thing you really have to have your family's support to do. You hop on the plane and you do this job or that job and then that job is finished. It's so flexible that you don't have to live in that particular city or that area to work."

The modeling gave her enough poise and confidence to enter the Mrs. Kansas pageant in 1989. She won the competition and went on to become the first runner-up in the Mrs. America pageant in Las Vegas. Before the national competition, she talked about how she had gotten where she was.

"I don't believe in luck. I believe luck is when preparation crosses the path of opportunity. So, I worked very hard to have these things come about and if they do, it's wonderful and if they don't, then I have my family. It's just the icing on the cake for me."

The pageants opened doors that Lou Ann never dreamed could be opened.

"The Mrs. Kansas (title) just led to some of the most wonderful experiences of my life. I never ever in my wildest dreams dreamed of getting that far."

As Mrs. Kansas she became, for about 800 miles, a copilot for an F-16 fighter jet and took part in tactical maneuvers at an air show in Russell and Salina.

Lou Ann also became a spokesperson for respite care and the Arthritis Foundation and worked with other charities. She talked to audiences about taking care of her younger brother, Sammy, who suffered from rheumatoid arthritis. The arthritis brought on complications with his heart and kidneys, and Sammy died at the age of 12, when Lou Ann was 16. Her mother had been the primary caregiver, but Lou Ann also took a share of the responsibility for tending him. Bringing out her story encouraged others fighting similar battles and, simultaneously, brought a benefit she had not expected.

Lou Ann shares a laugh with Cole, left, and Sammy, right.

"I've never been able to help in that kind of way. I felt like I made a difference. . . . It was healing. When you can help someone else, you become a better person yourself."

She has continued to work with those organizations, in addition to keeping up her modeling career and her family responsibilities. Lou Ann savors all aspects of her life.

"I don't try to live every day as if it's my last. I just try to cherish and make the most out of every day. Life's wonderful. I just try to live it to the fullest."

Ritchie with a display of past modeling assignments.

Snapshot Biography

Lou Ann Ritchie was born June 21, 1961, in Newton. She attended Newton High School, and married Jack Ritchie on Dec. 20, 1980, in Newton. They have two sons, Sammy, 10 and Cole, 7. Years in Kansas: 30.

Senior Ranchers of the Flint Hills

Matfield Green's Elizabeth and Wayne Rogler have deep roots in rolling hills

Elizabeth Rogler of Matfield Green is a child of the prairie. Born near Elmdale, she was the daughter of a second-generation Chase County farmer. But her career in home economics with the extension service took her to universities in Michigan, Indiana and Hawaii before she decided where she really wanted to be.

In 1954, she returned to Chase County and settled outside Matfield Green.

"I guess you're kind of born in open spaces and like to return. . . . I grew up in it, and I came back to it. I was on college campuses much of my life."

Elizabeth had another reason for returning to the Flint Hills. A friend of long-standing, Wayne Rogler, had asked that she come back and marry him.

"I was convinced to come home."

It was a decision she does not regret. Elizabeth owns 1,500 acres of the prairie; Wayne owns another 3,500. Together, they enjoy the peace afforded by the quiet, rolling hills.

"I guess if you've never seen or experienced open land such as we have here, it would be difficult to accept. It's just peaceful. Gets you away from the strains of our normal life. You have to adjust to the quietness out here. And, really, loneliness and isolation at times. If you learn to live with yourself, you're going to be all right."

Cattlemen and their families in that area know and help each other in ways that city dwellers sometimes cannot understand. Elizabeth Rogler does not find that familiarity unsettling. To her, it is a comfort.

"It's just plain friendliness. Everybody else knows your business. They know what you got for your cattle. There's nothing secretive out here. Everybody feels empathy for each other."

The Roglers, like other ranch families, know that the gently rolling hills with their plentiful bluestem grasses can be as harsh and unforgiving as they are calming and nurturing. In the Flint Hills, the prairie is law: It takes, it gives, and the rancher obeys.

"It looks like wasteland to a lot of people, I'm sure. I can say it must have been lonely to cross it the first time. I'm sure those hills must have looked about like this in 1859 when Grandfather Rogler came here. Maybe the grass was much higher. I think. . . the area has been very carefully nurtured over the years."

The Roglers are continuing that tradition, raising and grazing cattle on the hills. And together, they enjoy settling back to watch the sun set over the prairie.

"The sun is blinding. You just want to sit up and catch your breath."

"If you learn to live with yourself, you're going to be all right."

Snapshot Biography

Elizabeth Rogler was born April 1, 1912, in Elmdale. She earned a bachelor's degree in home economics from Kansas State University at Manhattan, a master's degree from Columbia University in New York, and did post-graduate work at the University of Chicago. She married Wayne Rogler on Feb. 2, 1954. Wayne Rogler was born on May 10, 1905, one mile north of Matfield Green. He attended Crocker Grade School and graduated from Chase County High School of Cottonwood Falls in 1922. He graduated from Kansas State University (then Kansas State Agricultural and Mechanical College) in 1926. Years in Kansas: Elizabeth, approximately 65; Wayne, 86.

He Couldn't Read Daughter's Name

Valley Center's Jimmy Runyan fooled bankers, but not his children

Success has blessed Jimmy Runyan of Valley Center, but it did not come easy. He and wife Carla have five children and the family is close. He has borrowed up to $250,000 to buy rental houses and a tanning salon. He also does automotive body work.

Most of all, now he can read, and he is deeply involved in Literacy Volunteers of America, encouraging others to overcome illiteracy.

"Until about 1986 I couldn't read and I was hiding it so bad I didn't realize I was hiding. It made me feel stupid — I didn't feel very good about myself. I'll tell you how bad it was. My daughter's name is Amy. Only three letters, but I couldn't read that. I'm still working hard to learn but now I can read anything I want to so long as I don't have to read it too fast."

Jimmy believes there are several reasons that he got through the 10th grade at Wichita North High School without knowing how to read. His family, with seven children, moved a lot. He was born in Oklahoma. He was in 12 different schools by the time they moved to Wichita and he entered the third grade. The family then stayed put. Jimmy attended Waco Elementary, Horace Mann Junior High and North High until he was "kicked out" at age 17.

When he should have been learning to read, schools were teaching the "sight" method in which children were to look at words as a whole, remember them and thus be able to read.

"I couldn't remember the words. I just had no way of knowing what I was supposed to be reading. One teacher swatted my hand because I couldn't read, and I just got belligerent. In math

they would break down the numbers, but when they were teaching reading, they didn't break down the words. Nobody in school did anything. They just passed me from one grade to the next."

Jimmy found ways of coping and faking. On multiple-choice tests, he just guessed, and the laws of chance helped him get by. When he got out of school, his street smarts helped him. He and Carla married in 1976, and she could read for him but she didn't understand the intricacies of contracts.

When Jimmy met with bankers, he carried off the charade so well they never thought he couldn't read, and he got the loans he needed as well.

"So I would just look like I was reading a contract and would ask a lot of questions. They would answer and I'd know everything about the contract. I never worried about being cheated and I never was."

Carla and Jimmy's children are Jeff, 14; Amy, 13; Derrick, 12; Lisa, 11; and Tammy, 6. When the older ones started school, Jimmy couldn't read notes teachers would send home. And when they started learning to read, he began to want to quit hiding and start learning, too. Once before, when he was 20, he paid a tutor $35 an hour to teach him to read.

"But I didn't stick with it. I wouldn't work at it. For a long time I thought somehow I could just snap my fingers and be able to read. But I hated not knowing how to read. I couldn't even look up things in the phone book. I couldn't write checks. You know how people say, when they're giving you directions, 'just go a couple of blocks and turn; you can't miss it.' You can miss it if you can't read street signs."

Runyan helps son Derrick, 12, study. He has 5 children.

Then he saw a television program on literacy and became convinced he, too, might learn to read. He hired another tutor, and this time he worked hard, studying for an hour or two each night.

"When I started, my 5-year-old daughter could read better than I could. I started reading first-grade books, then I was in second-and-third grade books. Finally, I said, 'Hey, I can read!' That was the big thing, to convince myself that I can read."

After two years, he got his general equivalency diploma. He is a member of the Wichita Area Literacy Foundation board and the statewide Alliance for Literacy. He now has attended three National Literacy Congresses in Washington, D.C., where he met Barbara Bush. After attending his second congress, he came home and started a student literacy group. He makes a lot of public appearances, talking about the importance of knowing how to read. And Jimmy is now serving as a tutor to a 49-year-old man.

"I talk to students about the importance of education to help you get a good job. I tell them, don't be more worried about getting that first car. Be worried about your life. I am not afraid to say I once couldn't read. Sometimes people will start trying to read stuff for me, but I just tell them, 'Hey, I can read it.'"

Carla used to write the checks for their business. Now Jimmy takes pride in writing all the checks. He fills out the tax forms and prepares end-of-year reports for the accountant. And he continues to press the boundaries of reading.

"I'm into phonics. For the longest time I didn't know that 'ph' sounded like 'f,' I didn't know that 'ight' was 'ite.' I keep on learning. And now I feel good about myself."

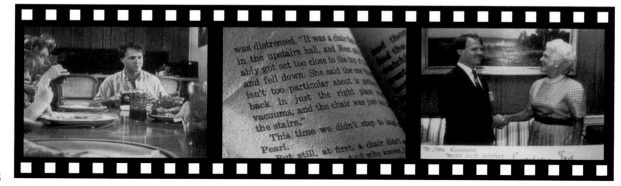

"My daughter's name is Amy. Only three letters, but I couldn't read that."

Snapshot Biography

Jimmy Runyan was born Jan. 13, 1958, in Oklahoma. He married Carla Posey in May 1976. They have five children. Years in Kansas: 25.

Jimmy Runyan – no longer faking it.

Bringing Dead Trees Back to Life
Gino Salerno treats Wichitans to wood sculpture in the parks

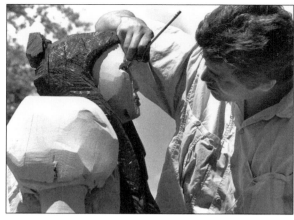

Mighty trees that once stood tall and proud have become a canvas for a Wichita artist's saw. The artist, Gino Salerno, has been commissioned by the Wichita Parks Department to carve sculptures from tired and broken trees.

Gino, a native of Lima, Peru, came to Wichita eight years ago to study fine arts at Kansas Newman College. He later ended up getting a degree in library science from Emporia State University.

Although he now has a full-time job as branch librarian at Minisa Library, his heart is in his art.

"For me, art is life, or life is art actually."

The tools for this art are rough and loud — a chainsaw, circular saw, sanders, other power tools, then chisels and hand tools for the finishing work.

"My tools are an extension of my arms, I can say that. They are like extra fingers there, to do the job right."

As with many artists, the economic realities limit this desire for expression. His work for the parks department is in the evenings and weekends, and he rarely has time to work on a long list of requests for privately commissioned work. But someday he would like to be sculpting full time.

One advantage of the library job, though, Gino says, is spending time in his favorite part of the library, "where all the sculpture books are."

Some of the nearly 20 of Gino's pieces adding a flair to Wichita's parks and river areas include: the "Woman and Dog," the female "Jogger" in Riverside Park, the "Clown" in McAdams Park and the "mail lady" near downtown.

The sculptures are sometimes impressions of people, and other times are more direct, such as the mail carrier on McLean Boulevard north of Douglas.

"It's based on the Minisa mail lady, and she loved it."

And there are very serious ones as well, such as the haunting sculpture called "Heart of Stone," or the unforgettable "Face of the Homeless" standing silently in one park.

"Working in the park has given me exposure to a lot of people who stop by and ask me questions."

Gino started with wood sculptures four years ago after working with small carvings. He approached the park board and officials agreed to let him do one tree. The park officials liked it, hired him on a part-time basis, and the rest is history.

Gino says there are only a handful of other artists in the nation he knows of who are doing this kind of public art. And he says Wichitans should take notice of not only his art, but many others as well. Too often, inflated value is given to the work of California or New York artists, he believes.

"There is a lot of good art in Wichita. I wish some of the people that buy art would select more local artists."

Artists have used wood for centuries because of its great beauty, texture and grain. And because it was once alive, artists feel a kinship. One piece Gino did privately, a 10-foot crucifix of Christ that weighs more than 300 pounds, was made from a walnut tree at a friend's home.

"The tree already had the branches in the shape of the arms. I saw the tree and had the idea of the crucifix immediately."

The quality of the wood is important ,too. Gino notes that totem poles in Alaska have lasted more than 800 years, but adds that there, termites and ants aren't a problem.

In 1990, Gino began work on a Wizard of Oz display in Watson Park in south Wichita. It includes the Scarecrow, the Tin Man, the Wicked Witch, Dorothy, Munchkins, a Yellow Brick Road and a tornado.

Most of the trees in the Oz collection were felled by the inland hurricane that hit Wichita and much of central Kansas on June 19, 1990. Salerno takes satisfaction that he is creating something to bring pleasure out of all the destruction that occurred that day when winds in excess of 100 miles an hour battered the city.

But recently, Salerno's own works of art have taken a battering. Vandalism to the Oz display forced the park board to hire a guard at night. Sculptures at other parks also have been hit. Vandals decapitated one, threw blue paint on another, and still others have been carved or written on.

Each time, with great patience, Salerno has repaired the damaged work. Though it's hard to understand what kind of person would destroy public art, Gino sticks with it, exercising large amounts of patience, persistence and forgiveness.

Despite the vandalism, Gino views Kansans favorably.

"They're friendly and caring, and there's more opportunity here."

Gino Salerno has already given much back to his adopted city. And he has big plans for the future. There's a three-ring circus on the horizon, complete with clowns, lion tamers and acrobats. And then there's that sketch he has of Noah's Ark . . . .

Gino Salerno with a few of his wooden "Oz" friends in Watson Park in south Wichita.

Snapshot Biography

Gino Salerno was born Oct. 14, 1962, in Lima, Peru. He graduated from high school there, then attended the Federal University of Pelotas in Brazil. He came to Wichita, where his brother lived, in 1983, and graduated from Kansas Newman with degrees in biology and fine arts. He received a master's degree in library science from Emporia State University in 1990. He and his wife, Marsha, were married on Jan. 1, 1987. Years in Kansas: 8.

Kansas Teenage Country DJ
Tammy Kay Schloterbeck livens up airways at Eureka's KOTE-FM

Many in the listening audience to KOTE-FM in Eureka have no idea that the sweet and mellow weekend country DJ from nearby Hamilton has only three years in the business, or that her voice was first heard on the airwaves when she was only 14.

And for those who do know how young she is, it doesn't seem to matter, because Tammy Kay Schloterbeck knows what she's talking about — country music. She also doesn't sound like a teenager. Some listeners have even told station officials they thought she was in her 20s.

"Here's 'Sweet Dreams' by Patsy Cline. . . . Hello, Greenwood County and Eureka! It's 4 after 5 and you're listening to KOTE, Eureka. I'm Tammy Kay and I'll be keeping you company country style, playing Coyote (KOTE) country classics until 7. Here's Jim Reeves and 'Four Walls'."

Self-motivated, enthusiastic and proud of what she's doing – that's Tammy Kay.

"I've always liked country music. I was excited when I heard that they were going to have a station and wanted to know if I was interested."

Tammy Kay first went on the air in October 1988, when KOTE made its debut from the cramped quarters of a converted mobile home outside of Eureka. Although the signal has since been boosted, the station is still housed in the same facility. Brothers Chris and Jay Brown own the station.

"She's very knowledgeable," said Jay, general manager for the country station that has a reach almost to El Dorado. "And she's very popular, too."

It was more of a case of being polite that the Browns decided to give Tammy Kay an interview.

"I knew her cousin and he mentioned her and said she had an ambition to be a country DJ," Jay said. *"I just shrugged and said, 'Yeah, and I want to be a fireman, too.' He convinced me she was serious and had a terrific knowledge of music and desire.*

"I had her come in and all of that was true, and she's been on the air ever since."

As to how she is perceived by listeners, Chris, who is operations manager, said most don't realize her age.

"She's actually more mature than a lot of 25-year-olds," he said.

The senior at Hamilton High School has been a fan of country music since grade school. She spends a lot of time building up her knowledge of the industry.

"Mostly I keep up by listening, reading album covers, magazines, and watching The Nashville Network . . . . I think the hardest thing for me is trying to decide which song to play."

KOTE is the only station in the whole county, so Tammy Kay's voice is well known. When she first went on the air, friends were very supportive, she said. Many viewed it as a novelty, but "not as much any more," she said. Her 7-year-old brother, Mike, though, "thinks it's kind of cool."

In the summers, Tammy Kay works at her father's machine shop in Hamilton and does her show on KOTE. Though she enjoys being on the air, her career may

Tammy Kay discusses her country music program with Jay Brown, general manager.

take another turn. First, she plans to go to college.

"Then, if I stay in it, it's more likely to be on the business side of it."

Who are her country favorites?

"I play old and new country. Some of my favorites are George Strait, Patty Loveless and Garth Brooks."

But she also likes Kenny Rogers and Ronnie Milsap. Her likes in school include drama and forensics, and her time is further limited by her participation on the volleyball team and as a member of the "quiz bowl team." All of that keeps Tammy Kay busy, and yet she still maintains a grade average that ranks toward the top of her class.

Tammy Kay said she was confident, but edgy the first time she went on the air. Now she enjoys it and is comfortable sharing her musical knowledge and talking with listeners.

So the next time you're in the Flint Hills, spin the dial over to KOTE 93.5 FM, and let Tammy Kay keep you company, country style.

Snapshot Biography

Tammy Kay Schloterbeck was born Dec. 31, 1973. She is a senior at Hamilton High School. Her parents are Donald and Barbara Schloterbeck, and she has a brother, Mike, 7. Years in Kansas: 17.

Choosing Chickens over Rocking Chair

Claude Schwab of La Crosse pursues an unusual heaven

Chickens and other farm fowl have been a major part of life for Claude Schwab of La Crosse since he was four and his father opened Schwab Hatchery and Feed Co.

Now 79, Schwab is contemplating selling or closing out the business that has provided millions of baby birds to farmers all over Kansas who raise the chickens, turkeys and guineas for their meat. But it is more than a business to Schwab. He talks with the birds and respects their personalities and their skittish natures. Before entering the guinea house, he knocks on the door.

"If I just walk up and open the door, they'll hit the ceiling. They're scared."

Cuddling and stroking a big rooster, he croons:

"This is the best old rooster in the state of Kansas, aren't you? You can make any of them like that if you take just a little time with them, and as long as they know you're going to treat them nice."

The hatchery and the feed store are in two buildings next to the Schwabs' home in La Crosse. Both are painted tan with darker brown trim. Last year, about 183,000 birds hatched and were sold from those buildings, which form one of the few hatcheries in western Kansas. They used to produce twice as many back when smaller farms filled the Kansas country-side and demand for fowl was so great that the Schwabs scheduled hatchings twice a week. Now they hatch once a week during the season, January through July.

The business started on the family farm north of town, but Claude's father moved it into La Crosse in 1928. Claude grew up working with the birds and

selling feed, and in the 1950s he bought the business. The original building on Highway 183 in La Crosse burned in the middle of the night in 1959 and they bought new equipment and built on land next to their home.

This makes it easy for Claude to check on the incubators in the middle of the night, as he must, and to visit with the birds, as he likes to do.

Genny, who is two years younger than her husband, grew up in nearby Bison. They married in 1932 and soon she was helping by "egg layering." She worked with Claude until about five years ago when her health forced her to stop. But the fowl needn't look to her for the same affection they get from her husband.

"I really think I take second place to them. He likes to talk with them, be with them. He gives them names, holds them on his knee. I don't feel like that. I kind of like them when they are little and fluffy. But they are kind of flighty when they are big, and I don't care for that."

But she still goes with him when he drives the van through western Kansas making deliveries. In season, Claude works seven days a week, 12 hours a day. He breeds his own birds and it takes a lot of work to turn an egg into a healthy chick delivered to a customer.

"You have to set the eggs and keep them separated. You put them, 180 eggs to a tray, in the incubator and 21 days later they hatch. The chicks then are put in boxes of 100, divided in quarters, and left to dry for half a day. Then you have to sort them by sexes and fill orders."

Some chicks are sent by mail, some are delivered,

some are kept in brooders until the buyers pick them up. When the season is over, the Schwabs are out of birds – they even sell the breeding stock. Then it starts all over again. But next summer, it may not. The Schwabs plan to close up by the end of the next hatching season.

They hope to sell, and hope the new owners will need Claude to initiate them into the business. That way, he could keep his hand in, and a fond eye on, the fowl.

"I sure wouldn't want to go sit in a rocking chair. I'd rather fall over dead. I want to go to chicken heaven. Go with my birds."

"I want to go to chicken heaven."

Claude Schwab shows off one of several thousand ducks hatched at his hatchery over the past year. Along with ducks, Claude also raises chickens and guineas, with total fowl numbering over 185,000.

Snapshot Biography

Claude Schwab was born in rural La Crosse August 6, 1912. He graduated from La Crosse High School and took various short courses at Kansas State University. He married Genevieve "Genny" in 1932. They have three daughters: Darla, who lives in LaCrosse; Billie Dawn, in Green Bay, Wis.; and Joy, of Newton. There are 11 grandchildren and 18 great-grandchildren.Years in Kansas: 79.

Pianist for a Bygone Era

Neola's Fred Sherman started playing for movie houses when he was 14

Fred and the elevator he's owned since 1942.

A few homes and an elevator are all that are left in Neola. But Fred Sherman is still there — has been for all but a few months of his 86 years — and it is his piano that keeps the elevator alive.

Fred bought the town's elevator in 1942, but he's probably better known around these parts for his years as piano player in the area movie houses. The elevator is no longer filled with grain, but it's still filled with music, thanks to Fred's storing of a piano there and his favorite afternoon pastime of tickling the ivories for old cronies.

"I go over for a couple of hours. We keep some pop on hand. A couple of loafers come over."

His favorites are the tunes he banged out during the Indian chase scenes and the tinkly melodies he played during the love scenes. He started playing the piano for the movies when he was 14 and had stints in movie houses in many of the surrounding towns — back then even tiny Turon had two theaters.

Growing up, Fred's house was filled with the music of his dad and grandfather, both old-time fiddlers. From the age of 8, he'd watch them play, and then he became interested in the pedal organ in the house and would walk barefoot the few miles to his music lessons.

"If you've got music in ya, it's gonna come out some way."

His lessons, though, were mostly classical music, and the first chance he got he started collecting sheet music. His pay was 50 cents a night for playing in movie houses in four surrounding towns. He supplemented that by organizing a band that played for dances.

Fred was born three miles from where he now lives in Stafford County, and his growing-up years were spent at towns that are just specks on the map: Turon, Zenith, Sylvia, Preston and Penalosa (population now 31), where he met his future wife. The biggest he can remember Neola getting was when he was 5 years old and it had two stores.

The trains don't even stop at Neola anymore, but Fred's content to let them go by. It's always been that way, except for the time he was 17 years old and hopped on board for an adventure to Wichita (he had to borrow $3 to get back home) and the time he spent the winter in Texas.

"Well, if you're a country person, it's just as near heaven as you can get on earth."

Then 22 years old, Fred patiently waited for his wife to finish high school and they were married two weeks later in 1928. It makes him happy that all but one of his two daughters, seven grandchildren and nine great-grandchildren live within a 100-mile radius of Neola.

"The farthest away is Hays except for the one in Little Rock, Ark. So many families are scattered."

Fred's a great storyteller and any lulls between piano numbers are filled with jokes. He's even been known to brag about the fact he's only been in a bathtub once since he was 18. (What he doesn't tell the audience is he prefers sponge baths instead.)

"I tell you what, I'll put my smell up against anybody who comes along."

Music is still a big part of his life and his group — Fred Sherman and Friends — still plays for senior centers and retirement communities. The youngest is about 70 and the group includes a violin, bass fiddle, slide trombone and mandolin. When there's no piano, Fred plays the accordion.

"One thing I live for now is to go around to these rest homes."

"If you've got music in ya, it's gonna come out some way."

136

Snapshot Biography

Fred Sherman was born Jan. 26, 1905, in Stafford County. He attended Stafford County schools and married Geneva in 1928. They have two children – Estol Coen, Florence Holmes – seven grandchildren, nine great-grandchildren. Years in Kansas: 86.

Fred Sherman, letting the music come out.

He's No Stiff, But the Ties Are

Harper's Paul Shue turns wood into talk-generating novelties

Paul Shue of Harper makes items from wood that make people talk. Only a few people in Kansas know about his work, though. While he looks for markets in this area, his collapsible wooden baskets and thin wooden neckties already are selling — almost faster than he can make them — in Pennsylvania and Chicago and Seattle and at major craft shows around the country.

"It looked like a hobby to me, but it's turned into a job."

Paul is a carpenter by trade, and when the carpentry business slowed down a few years ago he decided to try his hand at the wooden novelties, in addition to the shelves and rocking chairs and specially ordered items he was beginning to make in his shop. The job change jolted his concept of what work was.

"I felt guilty just sitting here at home in my shop, 50 feet from my house. It looked like a hobby to me, but it's turned into a job. I'm doing it really to make a living. I plan to continue on when I reach retirement age."

The baskets that he saw in Colorado and taught himself to make in his workshop seem to confound people. The art of making them, he says, lies in the cutting.

"They can't figure out how it works. When you go to a show with them, you hear a lot of adjectives: incredible, amazing, just different."

Paul spotted the ties in a Nashville, Ind., specialty shop where he was selling his baskets.

"My wife wouldn't let me buy one because they were so expensive — they were $74. Then, she bought one for me when I wasn't looking."

He took the tie home, taught himself how to make one and altered a couple of mistakes the craftsman had made: The knot on the tie was the same thickness as the tie itself instead of thicker, as a real tie is, and the stripe on the knot went the same direction as the stripe on the tie. It shouldn't have,

Paul said. He was satisfied with the results of the changes and so were the store owners and people who attend the crafts shows.

"The guy that was making them has quit . . . so they're buying from me and I'm real pleased. . . . I sell a boatload of 'em back there. I've got more stuff to make than I can think about doing."

Now his ties are legendary. Mike Hayden, when he was governor, even wore one on Arbor Day in 1990.

Paul's wife, Mary, helps out in the workshop. She measures and marks the wood to show Paul where to cut. She laughed about her role in the workshop, as she drew the rounded lines for a basket and hoped she had them in just the right spot.

"This is one place he always has the upper hand. When he says I shouldn't have done it that way, I shouldn't have done it that way."

And while the baskets are fascinating, Paul's leather-backed, flexible ties are guaranteed to generate comment around the office.

"You do have to treat them for termites once a year and watch out for woodpeckers."

Grandchildren Erin and Sara Crosthwait admire grandpa's handiwork.

138

"It looked like a hobby to me but it's turned into a job."

Snapshot Biography

Paul Shue was born April 22, 1931, in Gettysburg, Pa., and attended Biglerville (Pa.) High School. He married Mary Weaver on Sept. 3, 1950; they have four children– Brenda Jean Crosthwait, Bradley Paul Shue, Terry Wayne Shue and Timothy Dean Shue – and nine grandchildren. Years in Kansas: 21.

Mary Shue marks the bowls before Paul cuts them.

He's A Real 'Cop Reporter'

Argonia's Robert Taylor hands out warning tickets in his column

People in Argonia and Conway Springs don't gnash their teeth over crime reports. They chuckle. That's because Argonia Police Chief Robert "Pat" Taylor writes day-by-day crime reports every week in the *Conway Springs Star-Argonia Argosy.*

The 51-year-old one-man department formerly was a Wichita policeman for 23 years. He laces his column with laconic humor.

For example: "July 7 - Sheriff's office reported receiving call that Sumner County was being attacked by two Soviet MIGs. . . . I contacted one crop duster from the Argonia airport, but he was not aware of any activity. I am sure glad that it was a false report because it would have really upset harvest if it had been true."

Or "May 10 - Report of cattle out north of Argonia. Found a black bull eating grass in the ditch . . . . When I yelled at him over the loudspeaker, the bull cleared the fence very casually by at least two feet. Should be trained in steeplechase. Is as light-footed as a deer."

"A lot of little towns expect their police to make their pay by writing tickets. Argonia isn't like that. I write very few tickets. If I write about cattle or horses being out, pretty soon a farmer will be out fixing fences. Farm kids get their drivers' licenses when they are 14 and they drive in town to school. It's my job to see that they obey all the rules. If I write about a kid goofing around town in a red Mustang, pretty soon you may see that kid riding the school bus for a week. It means his dad read the column, checked into it and the kid is being punished."

Pat never names names and his column never pokes fun at sensitive subjects, such as sex crime. But many times he sees the ludicrous side of a serious problem, for example the costly damage caused by squirrels chewing on utility lines.

"July 23 - An Argonia squirrel climbed a pole behind Eldon's Automotive, and managed to shut down the electricity for the city for a few minutes. Fortunately, one squirrel does not last long when transmitting 3,400 volts. The electricity came back on when it ran out of squirrel to ground out."

After retiring from the Wichita Police Department, Pat took the job in Argonia, population 529, in 1987. Five or six months later the *Argosy* editor asked if he would write a column.

"The owner told her it would never go. But people liked it, and almost instantly they got a lot of new subscriptions. People in Conway Springs read it, too, and a great many people have moved away from Argonia; they subscribe to see what's going on."

A lot of people had a hand in teaching Pat to recognize human-interest stories and to write them.

"When I was a rookie, one particular policeman made me write all our reports, and he graded them. My writing was honed pretty well at Friends University, where they make you do a lot of writing. A reporter for KFH radio in Wichita, Fred Huddleston, would ask what was going on. I could tell him about three murders and he would pass them up for a report on two guys from McConnell that we picked up on East Douglas. They had cap pistols in shoulder holsters and they were scaring people."

Pat, who learned police basics in three years in the military, was head of intelligence in the Wichita department before he got into trouble for busting too many massage parlors, he said.

"I never knew how many people with influence patronized those places. Pretty soon I was made night jail supervisor."

There he became known for his 7:05 a.m. conversations with Nelson Shock, a KFDI radio reporter.

"He'd say, what's going on? I might tell him, 'Well, they brought in five or six prostitutes off South Broadway. We've got some men arrested for soliciting police decoys for prostitution and their wives are lined up out there to bond them out of jail. And we have several DUIs; you can hear some of them yelling back there.'"

Some supervisors were angered but Pat kept up the irreverent reports for five years until Shock died of leukemia and his successor "I guess couldn't stand the heat from the department." The reports died quickly.

Pat, his wife, Mary Lou, and three of their children moved to Argonia and like it. The children at home are Laura, a senior at Argonia High; George, a 10th grader; and Kathleen, an eighth grader. The others are Robert, a special agent with the U.S. Border Patrol in San Diego, and Mary Elizabeth, who teaches disadvantaged fourth graders in Little Rock, Calif.

"My blood pressure went down right away when we came here. I'm happier with myself and my family is a lot happier. The job takes about 280 hours a month but there's not a lot of hard work. We're sitting very well here in the community."

That isn't to say he plans to stay forever. He and Mary Lou carefully weigh ideas about moving to a larger police department, taking up another profession or even, as is frequently suggested, writing a book. But for now he is keeping a close eye on Argonia and its neighboring farmlands, and writing his weekly column.

Taylor talks with Ruth Harper, great-grandmother to many of Argonia's teens.

Snapshot Biography

Robert "Pat" Taylor was born July 24, 1940, in Milwaukee, Wis., and moved to Cheney when he was five. He and Mary Lou married in 1961 and have five children. He attended Cheney High School and earned a bachelor's degree in history and sociology from Friends University. Years in Kansas: 43.

Saving Some Old Friends from Ruin

Lehigh's Ike Thiessen has a garage full of restored memories

Ike Thiessen of Lehigh is a man who has spent his retirement with old friends – friends who were saved from ruin by Thiessen himself, a man in touch with the past.

The old garage that holds his 10 old friends – nine Fords and one 1929 Plymouth – evokes memories of past generations, when those old cars were new and Henry Ford was making history.

Decades ago, when Ford was still a young man, the old garage was the Ford Garage. Now it's Ike's with his black ghosts of the past.

"In 1909 came the revolutionary Model T. Seventeen hundred were produced in that first year. A miracle of mass production for that time."

Ike Thiessen remembers those times.

"I grew up with these cars. My dad bought one in 1920. In those days you could buy it for $300 and then you could get a battery and a starter with it."

The walls of the garage are decorated with hubcaps of all sorts from a variety of cars and trucks.

"You can go to these farm sales and buy a whole bunch for a dollar."

Thiessen bought his cars at farms from Texas to North Dakota, during the days when he and his family traveled as a custom-cutting crew until he retired in 1981. He'd find old Fords in barns along the way, make arrangements to buy them, then haul them home later on a trailer.

About five years before he retired, he began restoring them and, during the past 10 years, has devoted several hours each day to his hobby.

"I don't do 'em as perfect as a lot of guys do, but I have fun doing it . . . . You have to go for coffee too."

Like the custom-cutting business, the family pitches in to help.

"We all kinda enjoy it. I think probably it's interesting for the whole family. My sons-in-law, they're really into it too."

Thiessen needs no help getting the cars running; he already had years of experience maintaining his cutting equipment.

"I've got them all to running. They're not all perfect, but they're running. That's the easiest part."

And he does some body work and painting too. The upholstery work is saved for a friend who lends a hand occasionally in the restoration projects.

His wife, his son and some grandchildren show the cars off in parades around the Lehigh area. The storms the old cars have weathered no longer show. Now, in the autumn of their lives, they help Ike Thiessen pass the time in his.

"It's just been interesting to do, something to do. You've got to keep busy. When you enjoy it, that's not too bad."

Thiessen polishes one of the "10 old friends" that fill his garage.

Snapshot Biography

Ike Thiessen was born Oct. 18, 1912, at Inman. He attended Little Valley township school in McPherson County and the German Academy and Bible School at Inman. He married Helen Warkentin on June 9, 1935, at Lehigh; they have five children – Joyce, Arlene, Carol, Karen and Paul – 13 grandchildren and four great-grandchildren. Years in Kansas: 79.

Shining Shoes More Than a Business

Spencer Tolbert molds and touches lives from small Wichita store

It's not in the best part of town, and it's not the most modern shoe store. If you go by, you have to be looking for it and driving real slow just to find it. But the outside and the inside of the crowded store don't tell the whole story.

It's Spencer's Shoe Service on East 13th in Wichita. The business used to be called Sam Shustorman's Shoe Store when it was near downtown on East Douglas.

Spencer Tolbert has owned and operated the business since 1981, and you'll find him inside the store at least 12 hours a day, sometimes 15 hours.

Not unusual, you say. Well, you wouldn't say that if you met 70-year-old Spencer and some of his 11 children, all of whom have worked in the store at some time in their lives.

"I try to teach the kids responsibility and respect for other people."

Spencer sells new and used shoes, and repairs all shoes. And, he says, you can tell a lot about a person by what they wear on their feet.

"You can tell just about what kind of disposition they have, whether they turn them over, whether they're a slouch, or whether they're neat. Most people wear them until they fall apart, but they really should take them and keep them up."

Spencer's story is not on how many shoes he sells; instead, it centers on what he's given his 11 children.

Three of those children still work with him. They say he taught them how to work and, in turn, gave them a future.

One of his sons, Virgil, says of his father, "He always told us, if we wanted to eat, best to learn a trade, something to carry with us."

Another son, Anthony, puts it this way: "It's a gift he gave all of us, all my nine brothers. I like it. It's an art."

Spencer's children say he gave then a solid work ethic and a good outlook on life. And a good feeling about life is what you get when you meet Spencer.

And why does this man, who refuses to retire, who had five heart attacks in one day in 1986, look so good and feel so upbeat about life? Well, maybe all of us could learn from his routine.

He sleeps only three hours a night. Many days, he's at the store by 6:30 a.m. and leaves at 9 p.m. or later, although he does slip away for a few hours to check on the home front. He has been sick only a few days his whole life. The heart attacks kept him off work six days.

This endurance and strength have always been a part of the life of this native Wichitan. In the 1930s, Spencer was an amateur boxer, and tells of 91 knockouts. In high school, he starred in track.

"The reason I look so young is I try to keep in shape — I still push a mower, do a lot of chinups, and I walk fast — and because of my genes."

And what genes he has. His heritage is French, Irish, Arabic, Jamaican and Indian.

"I don't have just one race line, and I don't take any medications because my blood is so funny. I'm not African American. I'm American, a human being."

Spencer graduated from East High School in 1940. It was at East High, which was integrated, where he met some of his future customers, now elected officials and downtown businessmen who still regularly trek over to his East 13th Street store for a shoeshine.

Spencer married his first wife while still in high school, and worked as a janitor and ice cream maker at the Old Mill Tasty Shop in downtown Wichita. He began working for Sam Shustorman in 1940.

Spencer Tolbert helps granddaughter LaKeesha as she learns the art of shoe repairing. Sons Anthony, background, and Bruce, right, have worked in the store since grade school.

He moved to Denver and operated a shoe store there for 13 years, but returned to Wichita in 1963 because "Sam wanted me to come back." Sam died in 1972, and in 1981, Spencer bought the business from the family. He closed the downtown store in 1984 – because of rising property taxes and the "terrible" parking – and consolidated his business at the 13th Street location, where he had operated a separate business since 1965.

When the store was still downtown and still had the Shustorman name, some of the newer customers called him Sam. But that was all right with Spencer, as long as they left with a smile on their face and maybe a little jump in their step.

So the next time you're driving down East 13th in Wichita, glance over at Spencer's Shoe Service. It's a place where Spencer puts a lot of attention into each pair of shoes, and into seeing that his children get a good start on life, standing solidly on their own two feet. It's a place where you might hear him say:

"Every shoe's different. Every one is different."
Or: "I've learned you can love everybody; you just don't have to like them."

Snapshot Biography

Spencer Tolbert was born in Wichita on Dec. 9, 1920. His father died when Spencer was 11 months old. He attended schools in Iowa and Wichita, where he graduated from East High School. He was first married while in high school, and took a job at the Old Mill Tasty Shop in downtown Wichita as a janitor and ice cream maker. He had four sons from his first marriage: Spencer Jr., 52; Harvey Lee, 50; Larry 47; and Roger Dean, who died at the age of 29 in 1972. He and his wife, Velma, have been married 38 years, and have five children: Bruce, 37; Anthony, 36; Virgil, 34; Sherry, 33; and Janice, 29. He has two stepsons, Garland, 43; and Michael, 38. Spencer has 108 grandchildren and great-grandchildren. Years in Kansas: 50.

Jokes That Even Preachers Can Tell

Pilsen's priest, Arthur Tonne, fills 54 books with funny stories

Monsignor Arthur Tonne, formerly of Pilsen and recently moved to a new home in Marion, can't resist a touch of gentle humor, even when explaining how to pronounce his name.

"It rhymes with Johnny. Or, if you're a feminist, with Bonnie. But I don't care what you call me, just be sure to call me for supper."

Humor is part of the work of Tonne, who retired July 9, 1991, after 38 years as the parish priest in Pilsen and 59 years in the priesthood. He expects to find more time for his writing, which has produced 54 books, including nine volumes of *Jokes Priest Can Tell.* He has a new volume ready to publish when the inventory gets low enough to make it profitable. Each book contains at least 500 anecdotes, indexed and cross-referenced for easy use by the clergy.

"A little joke gets the attention of the people, helps them relax a bit and makes them more open to the Word of God. Not everybody approves. Some believe religion is a serious business and you have to be serious, and they think it is wrong to make people laugh in church. I can't imagine our Lord being like that. He was human, and I believe he liked to laugh. And the basis of all humor is inner happiness."

The monsignor finds his jokes everywhere – he hears them, reads them, and sometimes stories sent

by friends contain a gem. The jokes must help a minister make a point, lightly and memorably. They are used by ministers of many denominations.

"This is good: A grade-school teacher showed her class a picture of Whistler's mother, and asked the children to jot down their impressions about the painting. We've all seen that, a good old grandmother sitting in her rocking chair. One little boy wrote: It's a nice old lady waiting for the repairmen to bring back her TV set."

The monsignor has always liked a good joke.

"When I was on the 'David Letterman Show' he asked me where I got my sense of humor. I told him it must be in the genes. Both my mother and father had a good sense of humor."

In one book he poked fun at his own title.

"Naturally, monsignors are the butt of many good-humored jokes by their fellow priests. Recently the report – true or false – is making the clerical circuit that we now have an organization called MA, modeled after the well-known Alcoholics Anonymous. You guessed it. When a monsignor feels the urge to work, he calls another monsignor who is supposed to talk him out of it."

Tonne was born in Escanaba, Mich., to a Catholic mother and a father of the Moravian faith, who became Catholic while his son was in the Franciscan seminary in Cincinnati. Arthur Tonne took graduate studies at Catholic University in Washington, D.C., then taught high school. He came to Kansas in 1938 and for 13 years led the Newman Club at Emporia State University. In 1951 he moved to the Wichita Diocese and after serving in Little River for two years was assigned to Pilsen. He wanted the post so he could have more time for writing. In addition to caring for his parish of 560, he worked every day at his writing.

"After Mass each morning, I would read scripture and pray. Then I would have about two hours to write. My best time is from 9 o'clock on to midnight or later. I am a night owl."

He wrote his first joke book in 1953. His first book, written in the 1940s, was *Sermons with Parables.*

"I had been preaching in 22 different states.

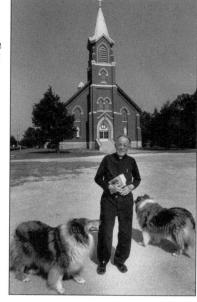

Pastors kept asking me if I had my sermons written down. I decided to write them. After preaching in the morning, I would write them down in the afternoon. That book was successful."

His most successful book has been *Five Minute Homilies on the Gospels of Cycles.* He is proudest, perhaps, of *The Story of Chaplain Kapaun.* It tells about Capt. Emil Kapaun, a Pilsen farm boy who was a hero of the Korean conflict because of his nurturing of fellow prisoners of war. He died in a North Korean prison camp in 1951.

"It took me a year to write. I got the idea of asking men who were in the POW camp with him to tell about Chaplain Kapaun. There were 82, of all nationalities. I found addresses for 72, and of those 48 responded. Their memories of the chaplain form the major part of the book; they are very touching."

Many of Tonne's books are out of print but the Kapaun memoir is available. In fact, he and his publisher are making a new effort to bring it to public attention. He currently is working on several new volumes, including *Push Up and Prayer,* on physical activity and prayer, and *Sermons with a Smile.*

In retirement he will be the support person for the two active priests in the parish.

"Without that, you write from an ivory tower. If you share people's tears, smiles, good luck, bad luck, you can approach them better. You can preach better, write better."

"After Mass each morning, I would read scripture and pray. Then I would have about two hours to write."

Snapshot Biography

Arthur Tonne was born July 4, 1904, in Escanaba, Mich. He attended parish schools, Franciscan Seminary in Cincinnati, graduate school at Catholic University, Washington, D.C.; he was named monsignor in 1960. His parents and his only brother, Lyle Philip Tonne, a mining engineer, are deceased. Years in Kansas: 53.

Rider of the Open Range

Bobbie Trayer tends 25,000 acres of Chase County ranch land

The prairie once stretched from Canada to the Gulf. No more. In Kansas, the Flint Hills are all that remain. Deep in those hills, near Bazaar, lives a woman dedicated to ensuring her portion of the hills endures.

Bobbie Trayer grew up in the area, helping her father and brother tend the Nation Ranch, a 7,000-acre piece of open range in the Flint Hills.

From him, she learned how to balance the needs of the range with the needs of the cattle. And she inherited a love of the land.

"I followed my dad around from the time I was big enough to get on a horse. It bothers me that other people don't appreciate the Flint Hills like I do. I love it here.

"It takes a certain type of person, I guess, to enjoy living out here. I have a lot of people ask me why I live out here and I guess it's just the place where I'm the happiest."

She had spent a few short intervals living in other states, but in 1974 the subtle but constant call of the hills brought her home for good.

"I guess I couldn't seem to stay away. I kept coming back and finally just decided I was going to move back and stick it out and see if I can't make a living on the place."

When Bobbie learned her brother planned to get out of the business, she volunteered to take over her dad's job as manager and gradually added another 18,000 acres to the land she oversees. That grassland is a seasonal home to up to 14,000 head of cattle each year. Both ranches are in Chase County.

"If we don't have the grass, we don't have anything."

Bobbie and her son, Chip, are partners in the business. Her husband, Charles, manages the Cottonwood Ranch 12 miles from the Nation Ranch.

In the busy season, their days begin before sunup and end long after sundown. Friends often remind her that she could do more managing and less "cowboying," but that is not what she chooses to do.

"It's hard work, living out here and running a ranch. It's a lot of hard work and long hours. But I sort of thrive on that, I think. . . I've always had the feeling that I can't ask somebody to do what I can't do myself.

"I kinda feel like I know what I'm doing here. I feel like I know how to take care of it."

That confidence was not always present. In the early years, she believed she needed to prove herself.

"I had to prove to everybody that I could do it. Back then, girls just didn't do that type of work. My dad did it right, and I wanted everybody to know that he taught me how to do it right."

If she needed any verification of her skills, she got it in 1991 at a meeting of the Grassroots Association, a group dedicated to preserving the Flint Hills. She recalled the way one of the ranchers introduced her at the meeting.

"He said, 'She takes care of the ranch like her dad did.' And that made me feel so good."

"I kinda feel like I know what I'm doing here. I feel like I know how to take care of it."

Snapshot Biography

Bobbie Trayer was born Nov. 1, 1938. She attended Matfield Green schools. She married Charles Trayer on Feb. 10, 1990, in a horseback ceremony deep in the Flint Hills. She has one son, Chip Hammond; and two grandchildren, Rope and Dalli. Years in Kansas: 40.

Animal Nurse and Social Worker
Mayetta's Louise Unrein provides care to injured, orphaned animals

A steamy afternoon in northeast Kansas . . . hot, muggy, a real lazy day. Lazy except for Louise Unrein, one of the human members on this 80-acre farm near Mayetta. Louise is a combination nurse and social worker. Her clients are animals. She is licensed by both the U.S. Department of Interior and the Kansas Wildlife and Parks Department.

Those licenses allow her to give special care to injured and orphaned animals . . . orphans, like mischievous Sammy the bobcat, who learned in his younger days that you don't mess with a domestic tabby. Fortunately for Sammy, the raccoon he plays with is more tolerant, and even lets Sammy pull on its tail.

On the Unrein place 20 miles north of Topeka, Louise and husband Louis share their corner of the world with dozens of wild and tame animals roaming the hills.

"My husband's very kind but he says I'm a real do-gooder. He said, 'If I'd mind my own business. . . .' But I think animals are my business."

Animals . . . she's got. Geese, pigs, mustangs, raccoons, donkeys, hawks, coyotes, dogs, cats and, of course, Sammy the bobcat. Amazingly, most of these animals get along, sharing the same yard, getting fed at the same time.

"My oldest son says, 'Mother, you can't save the world,' but if you don't try, than you might as well quit. You know, you got to keep trying.

"I know a lot of people won't agree with what I say, but I've put a lot of thought into this. I think there are worse things for animals than death."

Many of the animals Louise takes in have been badly treated by humans, dumped in the countryside and facing starvation, or injured, or even shot at.

"If people would see some of the wildlife that I get to take care of, or dogs and cats, the condition that they come in, death is good."

Animals like Sammy are lucky. But Louise says the responsibility for their care belongs to all of us.

Louise's approach to life extends over to her regular job of teaching sixth graders in nearby Hoyt. She's taught at the junior high and high school level, but prefers the age group she works with now because she can have more of an impact.

"I teach because I think if you just help one child it makes a difference. Children and animals are at the mercy of adults. If we don't have empathy for them, I think we're going to lose the children and all the animals."

Children play a big role in her life. She and her husband are raising two grandsons, orphaned when their father died when they were only 1 month and 1 year old.

"It's a wonderful experience for them. They help feed the animals. They are learning to have empathy and to care for all living things."

The Unrein place also has sparrow hawks, ground and gray squirrels, eagles, owls and songbirds. Sometimes zoos and wildlife officials bring her endangered species. Other times, the animals come from the humane society or from friends and acquaintances who know of her work. Some call after reading of her efforts.

The youngest animals, such as a 1-week-old fawn, and the injured, stay in a fenced yard and eat and sleep on the back porch.

Others roam in the wooded hills, or play near the

Louise gets help feeding a fawn from grandsons Michael, 7, left, and Daylon, 8, right.

pond or along the creek. When they're healed, many slip off in mating season, Louise says. They are protected at the Unrein place. Hunting and the use of herbicides are taboo. The 80 acres regularly draws two herds of deer that migrate through.

Some would say all this activity would wear on a person.

"You get tired, but you don't quit."

Even though she doesn't get paid for the care or the food, Louise will continue her work with animals. For her, animals like Sammy are not pets. They are her guests. And who knows, maybe through her work, she can change the world. It's worth a try.

Louise Unrein holds a baby possum that she is helping to raise on her farm near Mayetta.

Snapshot Biography

Louise Unrein was born June 12, 1927, in Manhattan. She graduated from Hugoton High School and attended Kansas State University, where she met and married her husband, Louis, in 1947. She left college to go to work, but returned to college in the 1980s, graduating from Washburn University in Topeka with a bachelor's degree in education. She and her husband, a retired electrical engineer, have lived near Mayetta for 17 years. They have three sons: Thad, 37, Topeka; Terry, 32, Houston; and Tim, 22, Newport, R. I. A fourth son, Ted, died in 1983. They are raising two grandchildren: Daylon, 8, and Michael, 7. Years in Kansas: 64.

Her Home-Cooked Meals Are Just $1

At Frances Ward's cafe in Yates Center, you make your own change

There aren't many places in this country where you can find a home-cooked meal for a dollar — including coffee or sun tea. And there's something even more unusual — and reassuring — in this small-town cafe.

"They make their own change. The cash register is never closed."

This doesn't concern proprietor Frannie Ward in the least; in fact, she has found that many of the more than 150 customers who crowd Frannie's Lunch Room each day leave more than the required dollar. And the fact that many pay the extra dollar for a piece of her pie guarantees that the 4-year-old Yates Center institution can afford to continue serving hundreds of locals and visitors every week.

Frannie cooks up only one menu selection each weekday, but her customers certainly don't complain. There's always the popular taco salad on Fridays, but the other days are dictated by whatever foods are on sale at the grocery store that week: some days there's chicken and noodles with mashed potatoes, and others there's meat loaf with baked potato or ham and beans with made-from-scratch cornbread. She's had to give up the popular fried chicken because it got too expensive. Her customers may miss it, but Frannie doesn't miss the frying that had to start at 3 a.m.

She usually climbs the 31 steps to the second floor of the downtown building which houses her cafe at 7 a.m. and begins dishing out the food at 10:30 a.m. She can serve 70 at a time — which includes using the picnic tables in the hallway — and serves until it's all gone. She then starts baking pies and getting ready for the next day's meal. If there's baked potatoes, it means scrubbing as many as 165 spuds.

Frannie's reputation rests as much on her friendliness as her home cooking.

"I try to take time and talk to people because they like it."

She banters good-naturedly with eaters and once even received a proposal of marriage.

" 'Frannie, will you marry me?' he said. 'Can I quit my job?' I asked. He said, 'No, I want you to start another one.' I told him to drop dead."

Frannie is particularly proud of her pies — rhubarb is the most popular — and they have traveled all over the country, from Las Vegas to New Jersey. The pies come in many varieties, from fresh peach to chocolate, and can be cut in seven generous wedges. She sells a whole pie for $5.

On Thursdays, visitors get an extra-special treat — homemade cinnamon rolls for 15 cents go on sale at 7:30 a.m.

"I do it just once a week so it's a treat for people."

Frannie does the week's shopping every Monday morning and her groceries run between $400 and $500, which will serve between 150 and 175 people every day. The Friday taco salad takes 45 heads of lettuce.

Why does she do it? She started the restaurant four years ago to help pay the bills when her husband, who died in 1990, was first diagnosed with cancer. But she continues for a different reason.

"I don't have anything to go home to. Last weekend I made 25 pies."

Instead of dwelling on her misfortune, however, the 60-year-old who's not afraid to wear tennis shoes with her skirts, pours her energy into her business, which she started with $5 borrowed from her granddaughter.

"And now this is all mine and I don't owe nobody nothing."

Her granddaughter helps with the work and Frannie has one paid employee and a volunteer who offered to help out one day and has been there ever since. Their lunches are served on real plates because it's cheaper to wash them than buy paper plates. Though she does it somewhat guiltily, Frannie gives herself the day after Thanksgiving off.

At the end of a long day of pie baking, chopping vegetables, cooking and serving, Frannie likes to relax and watch some baseball.

"The Royals are my team even though they're not doin' very well."

"I don't have anything to go home to. Last weekend I made 25 pies."

Snapshot Biography

Frances Ward was born May 1, 1931, in Buffalo. In 1948 she married Keith Ward, who died in 1990. They had three children: Dale Ward, Sherilyn Clarke, Rosan Williams; and three grandchildren. She returned to high school in later years and graduated fromYates Center High School in 1973 at the age of 42. Years in Kansas: 60.

Wichita's Quilting Queen
To Lillie Webb, sewing is more than just a hobby

There is nothing Lillie Webb of Wichita enjoys more than sitting down with her round quilting frame to make the tiny stitches that finish her handmade quilts.

"I just love to quilt. I've made more than 100 of them and lots of quilted wall hangings."

Lillie, who was born Feb. 1, 1909, grew up sewing and quilting, learning from her mother, Elva Hutcherson, and grandmother, Sarah Turner. They left her a legacy of about 10 unfinished quilts that she had to lay aside for all the years she was making a living to support her four children.

For 18 years she was a sewing instructor for Singer, teaching hundreds of people how to use their sewing machines. When she finally retired in 1971, she dug into that box, pulled out the quilts and finished every one. Then she started anew, making more quilts.

"I like scrap quilts. I love to work with the pieces, and they say I have a good eye. I'm not much for the pictorial quilts; I like the old-fashioned ones like the Double Wedding Ring or the Flower Garden."

Lillie is a member of the Prairie Quilt Guild, a Wichita group of enthusiasts who meet one Tuesday a month. Nothing tells her story better than the friendship quilt that guild members made and presented to her on her 76th birthday. The original pattern consists of lilies pieced from scraps of cloth. Her guild friends added their signatures and the quilt is inscribed, all the way around the border, with this message:

"For Lillie Hutcherson Webb, who was born in 1909 and who loved color, cloth and quilts before she can remember . . . who made her own clothes by the time she was 12 and who as a child helped her mother and grandmother make quilts and comforters . . . who sewed for others and taught it so well she was called the instructor with the golden touch . . . who made more than 70 quilts and who on her 76th birthday is given this Prairie Lily Friendship quilt by Prairie Quilt Guild members who admire her as a quilter, cherish her as a person and value the way she blooms, a true Prairie Lillie in their midst."

"I thought I was going to a quilt show at the Downtown Senior Center. I walked in and my friends were there, most of my children were there. I was so flabbergasted. There sat girls I had taught, friends from church. And that day my three girls played for me. I never thought I would hear them play together again. I burst into tears."

Lillie's daughters who dusted off their instruments for the event are Maxine McAllister, Wichita, marimba; Dorothy Haynes, Clearwater, guitar; and Beverly Neale, Salt Lake City, accordion. The "Prairie Lillie" event went on for three full days, and garnered coverage from national quilting magazines. Her work has been recognized in other quilting publications.

In the years since that heart-warming birthday party, Lillie has continued to add to her personal store of quilts and wall hangings. She also meets each Tuesday at Bethany United Methodist Church with a group of more than 30 women who make quilts and comforters for the needy.

"We have wonderful fellowship and we help a lot of people. I will mark the quilts, showing where to put in the stitches or ties. So many don't want to work the sewing machine, so I will do that too."

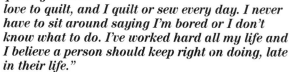

She works the sewing machine at home too, making clothes for herself and Maxine. And she sews her quilt pieces together by machine if possible. The Flower Garden and Inner City patterns, both consisting of tiny pieces in complex patterns, are two that have to be pieced partly by hand.

"But I always quilt by hand. I love to quilt, and I quilt or sew every day. I never have to sit around saying I'm bored or I don't know what to do. I've worked hard all my life and I believe a person should keep right on doing, late in their life."

She does have aches and pains. For example, when she sits and quilts for a long time she sometimes gets an unbearable pain in one foot. Her remedy: she gets up and mows the lawn or does other physical work.

Only rarely will she sell the quilted fruit of her labor. Her quilts and wall hangings will go to her four children, 10 grandchildren and 11 great-grandchildren and eventually to future generations.

"My kids would kill me if I sold my quilts. And besides, you can't make anything; most people don't realize the hours that go into a quilt. Not long ago I was talked into selling a little wall-hanging of the Inner City. I'm sure he thought he paid a good price – $125– but I put in 50 hours making it. Figure it out."

Lillie has lived in Wichita since 1940. After she and her husband separated, Lillie reared the four children by herself.

"It was hard, and one of the hard things was that I was so busy I just had to forget about quilting. But my children have been wonderful. I just couldn't ask for children who would treat me better."

Snapshot Biography

Lillie Webb was born on Feb. 1, 1909, and reared in Missouri, a half-mile from the Kansas line and 25 miles north of Fort Scott. There she attended a country school at Hume, Mo. After marrying on Oct. 28, 1928, the couple moved to Plains, and then eastern Kansas before moving to Wichita in 1940. She has three daughters, one son, 10 grandchildren and 11 great-grandchildren. Years in Kansas: 63.

Two Policemen Who Left the Fast Lane

Phil Williams and Jim Donovan chose life in Canton over California

Police chief Phil Williams and his partner Jim Donovan gave up the fast lane in California for the rural wheat fields of Kansas. They're the entire law enforcement department for Canton, population just under 1,000.

Williams is a 23-year law enforcement veteran, working most of that time for the Los Angeles police department. Donovan is a native New Yorker who worked for the police department in San Diego, where the two met. A lot of their co-workers were surprised at their decision to settle in such a rural community.

"They couldn't understand," Williams said. "But since then a lot have been looking at small towns."

Gang violence is something that's only read about here in rural McPherson County, where the two police officers are called by their first names. They regularly mingle with the locals over coffee at Cheryl's Cafe — which Donovan refers to as their substation.

Williams, a native Californian, had relatives in Kansas and had visited the state on family vacations. His three children ranged in age from four to 10 when the family moved to Canton.

"They love it, the freedom. They don't have to worry about gang violence."

Both Williams and Donovan and their families were quickly accepted by the community they now call home.

"I've been accepted into the community and it's now very comfortable," Williams said. "My family is happy and of course that makes me happy."

Williams took over as police chief in 1988 and then convinced Donovan to join him.

"He told me all about Canton," Donovan recalls. "How homey it was, how friendly. I knew all about them before I even got there," he said of the townspeople. "They were giving me hugs when I got here."

Donovan said he thought he was leaving warfare behind when he got home from serving in the Vietnam War, but he found equally as dangerous situations serving as a police officer in New York and California.

"I wanted my son to have what I did growing up," he said in explaining the reason for making the move to Kansas.

One of the biggest battles he's had to fight so far was against runaway cattle.

"I had one bull corner me behind a tree. I held up my nightstick and prayed he knew who was boss."

Though Donovan grew up in New York, it was in a small town, so the rural setting took little adjustment.

"I grew up in a town like this 30 years ago. This is a nostalgia rush for me."

But their jobs aren't as easy as it sounds. Williams is on call 24-hours-a-day and Donovan takes over on weekends.

But interspersed with the occasional break-ins and domestic disturbances, they find time for other important duties, says Williams.

"We unlock cars, there's a dog loose. The larger police departments don't even deal with that. The kids come up to you, dogs are important to them. Or you put a Band-Aid on 'em."

Taking care of Canton, Kansas, is a lot different than San Diego, where the calls to police must be answered by priority, says Donovan.

"This is not a major highway like we're used to patrolling," he said, pointing to Canton's quiet main thoroughfare. "It's wonderful here. I love Kansas and I'll never leave it."

Perhaps even more important than the routine patrolling is remembering to ask about a sick spouse or planning the law enforcement display for the annual county fair, Canton's local claim to fame. Or leading the All-School's Day parade in the county seat of McPherson on the Canton Police Department's new motorcycles.

And yes, there are the allusions to Mayberry and to Andy and Barney. But the two don't mind.

"They let me have more than one bullet," Donovan jokes.

"I had one bull corner me behind a tree. I held up my nightstick and prayed he knew who was boss."

Snapshot Biography

Phillip Williams was born Nov. 8, 1943, in San Diego. He graduated from San Diego's Helix High School in 1962 and attended Grossmont College, where he earned an associate's degree in 1965. He and his wife, Jackie, have three children: Patrick, 12; Brent, 9; and Erin, 7. Years in Kansas: 3. Jim Donovan was born March 21, 1948. He and his wife, Marilyn, have four children: Dawn Marie, 24; Jimmy, 22; Susan, 21; and Ian, 12. Ian is in school in Canton and Susan has returned to live with her family in Canton. Years in Kansas: 2.

Farmer of Memories
Charles Woolf of rural Cheney collects items with a history

There's one rural Sedgwick County man whose farm is a little different than most. Visiting Charles Woolf and listening to his stories of the past is like stepping into a time machine.

Charles still lives on the homestead four miles northeast of Cheney where he was born in 1915. His family has lived 105 years on the same land, which his grandfather bought from the original homesteader. He and Grace, his childhood sweetheart, have lived there since their marriage in 1936.

"It's a wonderful place to live and raise a family. Out here you do what you want, when you want to. You don't do that in the city."

But Charles doesn't till the soil. An accident 25 years ago kept him from farming the 200 acres. Instead, he farms memories, storing them for future generations in his barns. His old dairy barn houses everything from buggies to radios. The collection was

built piece by piece over the last quarter century. It even includes the doctor's instruments used to deliver him 76 years ago.

"I started small, got one piece, brought it home, refinished it."

It grew from there. It had to. Charles had to have something to take his mind off his injury.

"Well, I had to do something. I can't go fishing. Couldn't think about myself. You can't do that. I was paralyzed from the waist down. Well, I never had a hobby. I thought a hobby was a waste of time."

Not only did he find an avocation, he found thousands of historic items, tokens of Kansas' past he stores in barns at his rural Cheney farm.

Now those pieces number in the thousands. They hang from the ceiling and cover scores of shelves in the barns. Vintage radios still play, a Gem Roller Organ still turns out tunes, and toys and wagons are reminders of a bygone era.

Piece by piece, he added to his collection, which ranges from a switchboard to a complete barbershop. What they all have in common is they are a part of Kansas' past, just like the Woolf family.

Charles professes to have no favorites in the collection, though he's particularly fond of a very rare portable pantry that came from a covered wagon. Many of the items have stories behind them and he's quick to share them with the approximately 150 family and friends who have toured his collection.

Though the size of his collection could rival that of many museums, he seldom parts with an item, except if it's a duplicate. It's a little more difficult to get around at auctions now, but "a wheelchair will get ya there," he says. Prices are also higher now than when he started buying and he exercises a little more discipline at sales.

"I have just as much fun watching as buying. I used to have to buy something every time I went. I'm full up. I just play with what I've got."

Charles Woolf in the old-time barber shop he has re-created.

"Out here you do what you want, when you want to. You don't do that in the city."

Snapshot Biography

Charles Woolf was born on his family's farm near Cheney on Aug. 11, 1915. He and his future wife, Grace, grew up together, attending school and church in Cheney. They married in 1936 and have four sons — Stanley, Melvin, Gordon, Allen — and 10 grandchildren. Years in Kansas: 76.